KEELE
UNIVERSITY

CODES OF CONDUCT FOR ELECTIONS

A Study Prepared for the Inter-Parliamentary Union

by

Guy S. Goodwin-Gill

1998

CODES OF CONDUCT FOR ELECTIONS

Guy S. Goodwin-Gill

Inter-Parliamentary Union

Geneva

1998

ISBN 92-9142-039-5

Published by

THE INTER-PARLIAMENTARY UNION
P.O.Box 438
1211 Geneva 19
Switzerland

Produced with financial support from the
Swedish International Development Co-operation Agency (SIDA)

Layout, printing and binding by ATAR, Geneva, Switzerland
Cover design by Aloys Robellaz, Les Studios Lolos, Carouge, Switzerland

Table of Contents

FOREWORD   VII

PREFACE AND ACKNOWLEDGEMENTS   IX

1.	INTRODUCTION	1
	1.1 International law, obligations and implementation	1
	1.2 Purposes of a Code of Conduct for Elections	3
	1.3 Codes of Conduct and the promotion of 'peaceful elections'	4

2.	PRACTICE AND PROBLEMS	7
	2.1 Elections and finance	7
	2.1.1 Financing: Some dimensions to the funding question	9
	2.1.2 Financing and Code of Conduct issues	15
	2.1.3 Money and the means of communication	17
	2.1.4 Preliminary conclusions	19
	2.2 Elections and the media	20
	2.2.1 Role of the media	20
	2.2.2 Access to the media	22
	2.2.3 Balance and bias in the media	24
	2.2.4 Media responsibility and Codes of Conduct	27
	2.2.5 Compliance	29
	2.2.6 Preliminary conclusions	31
	2.3 Election observation	31
	2.3.1 Election observation and international law	31
	2.3.2 National observers	33
	2.3.3 Terms of reference	34
	2.3.4 Responsibilities and methods	37
	2.3.5 The rights and conduct of international observers	40
	2.3.6 Preliminary conclusions	43
	2.4 Elections and fair campaign practices	43
	2.4.1 The responsibility of political parties and candidates	45
	2.4.2 Restrictions on political activity and speech	47
	2.4.3 Preliminary conclusions	51

2.5 The institutionalization of electoral process   52
   2.5.1 Electoral commissions as 'best practice'   54
   2.5.2 Protecting the integrity of the system   56
   2.5.3 Preliminary conclusions   57

3.   A CODE OF CONDUCT:
   MODEL SCOPE AND CONTENT   59
   3.1 The potential scope of a Code of Conduct   61
   3.2 The potential content of a Code of Conduct   62

A MODEL CODE OF CONDUCT
FOR ELECTIONS   64

ANNEXES: CODES OF CONDUCT FOR ELECTIONS   73

SELECT BIBLIOGRAPHY   135

Foreword

"The will of the people shall be the basis for the authority of government; this will shall be expressed in periodic and genuine elections which shall be by universal and equal suffrage and shall be held by secret vote or by equivalent free voting procedures."

Set out in 1948 in the Universal Declaration of Human Rights, this principle has been not only taken up but also developed by the Inter-Parliamentary Union. For the world organisation of Parliaments, the key element in the exercise of democracy is clearly the holding of free and fair elections at regular intervals enabling the people's will to be expressed; but it is also essential that elections must be held in such a way that all voters can choose their representatives in conditions of equality, openness and transparency that stimulate political competition.

Not content with merely affirming this general principle, the Union has also worked to give it practical content. It therefore entrusted Professor Guy S. Goodwin-Gill with undertaking a study which it subsequently published in 1994 under the title *Free and Fair Elections : International Law and Practice*. On the basis of that study, the Council of the IPU adopted that same year, in Paris, a *Declaration on Criteria for Free and Fair Elections*.

Since their publication, the study and the Declaration have been reprinted several times and have been distributed in thousands of copies around the world, thus demonstrating that they responded to a widely felt need. Indeed, the Declaration has inspired and given substance to electoral reform in many countries and provided the basis for the monitoring and evaluation of many electoral processes.

Very recently, the IPU has emphasised the paramount importance of the right to organise political parties and carry our political activities[*]. It also believes that party organisation, activities, finances, funding and ethics must be properly regulated in an impartial manner in order to ensure the integrity of the democratic process.

Once again, the IPU wished to go beyond the mere affirmation of principles and offer tools for the improvement of national legislation and

---

[*] *Universal Declaration on Democracy* adopted by the Inter-Parliamentary Council in September 1997 in Cairo.

practice on the part of politicians. It therefore asked Professor Goodwin-Gill to pursue the earlier work which he had performed so ably.

The IPU is now pleased to present the results of his research. Entitled *Codes of Conduct for Elections*, it provides a comprehensive review of practical problems and solutions relating to financing of elections, media coverage, election observation, campaign practices and the institutionalisation of the electoral process. Skilfully combining elements of law and practice, the study also offers a model code of conduct and contains in annex a great number of texts which have served as codes in various countries.

In his introduction, Professor Goodwin-Gill has fittingly expressed his thanks to all those whose contributions have enriched the study, to which the IPU wishes to add its voice. The IPU also wishes to record its gratitude to the Swedish International Development Co-operation Agency for its important financial contribution which has made this study possible.

Professor Goodwin-Gill's study now offers a valuable source of reference to governments, bodies responsible for organising elections, political parties and the candidates themselves. The Union is very grateful to the author and hopes to have made a substantial contribution to the advancement of effective, fair and transparent electoral processes which will bring the world's peoples closer to the ideals of democracy.

Pierre Cornillon
Secretary General
Inter-Parliamentary Union

Preface and Acknowledgements

Even the casual reader will notice that the present short study takes up one of the themes touched on in *Free and Fair Elections: International Law and Practice*, published by the Inter-Parliamentary Union in 1994. The latter was largely limited in scope to a review of practice among countries in transition, either from war to peace or from one-party to multi-party systems. It was a study 'for the moment', capturing a particular time of peak interest in elections and their international dimensions, but together with the *Declaration on Criteria for Free and Fair Elections* adopted by the Inter-Parliamentary Council in March 1994, it also contributed to the debate about democracy and democratization.

At the same time, however, the Inter-Parliamentary Council wanted to go further, and to widen coverage of certain election-related issues to the established democracies. The intention is to look beyond the legislative and administrative framework, and to focus on the *conduct* of elections and *behaviour* in elections. If free elections are predominantly a matter of form, then *fair* elections are often a matter of substance. This Study is thus part of a continuing process of review of a number of current concerns, including corruption (a study of standards of conduct in public life will follow); the distorting effect of money on the electoral process; the responsibility (and irresponsibility) of the media; and fair and unfair campaign practices, such as negative advertising.

The Inter-Parliamentary Union is as troubled as many other organizations with falling interest and some cynicism among the public towards the democratic process and political life in general. The IPU is not a 'legislative' body, but it does promote co-operation and provide technical assistance, resources and expertise, and is also involved in standard-setting. In this sense, the IPU serves as a forum in which parliamentarians can promote principles and practice on behalf of parliaments and representative forms of government in general. It is hoped that, like the Study and Declaration on free and fair elections, the present work and the model Code of Conduct attached will contribute to the debate on standards, and either help to create or confirm certain expectations about the administration of and participation in elections.

Once again, it has been a pleasure to work with the Inter-Parliamentary Union. I particularly appreciate the strong personal interest and support of Pierre Cornillon, the Secretary General of the IPU, in this and in related work, as well as the unfailing encouragement, commitment and ready comments of Anders B. Johnsson, Deputy Secretary General of the IPU. The author has been fortunate indeed to have had such backing.

This Study has benefitted greatly, of course, from the work of many individuals and organizations associated with elections and the processes of democratization. A meeting on election observation and election administration, organized by the Office for Democratic Institutions and Human Rights (ODIHR) of the Organization for Co-operation and Security in Europe in Warsaw in April 1997, provided a timely opportunity to gather information and develop ideas. Thanks are due to Ambassador Audrey F. Glover, then Director of ODIHR, Eric Rudenshiold, Director of Programmes for the OSCE Parliamentary Assembly, to the staff of ODIHR and to the numerous participants with whom I was able to exchange views.

A first draft of this Study also drew helpfully on the comments of many others with crucial experience in the elections field. The International Federation for Election Systems (IFES) kindly and efficiently organized a review meeting in Washington D.C. in June 1997. Richard W. Soudriette, President of IFES, again gave his warm support to the project, and I am grateful to his colleagues, Jeff Fischer, George Jones, and Ray Kennedy for their views, to Sandra Shuster for arrangements and organisation, to Richard Smolka, Editor of *Election Administration Reports,* Dave Merkel, International Republican Institute, and Pat Merloe, National Democratic Institute, for their contributions, and to Quentin Wendt who acted as rapporteur. IFES continues to be a generous resource, and the practical knowledge of its staff is frequently relied on in the text that follows. Thanks are also due to Dr. Didier Maus, Director of the International Institute for Public Administration (IIAP), and Georges Bergougnous of the *Conseil constitutionnel (Service juridique),* who both provided the author with detailed written comments on aspects of French law and practice.

Notwithstanding the wide-ranging contributions to the present Study, the views expressed are those of the author, who remains responsible for any omissions or errors.

Guy S. Goodwin-Gill
Wolfson College, Oxford
October 1997

1. INTRODUCTION

1.1 International law, obligations and implementation

Article 21 of the 1948 Universal Declaration of Human Rights lays down the basic premises for 'election rights', later developed by article 25 of the 1966 Covenant on Civil and Political Rights to include, among others, 'the right *and the opportunity*', to take part in the conduct of public affairs, directly or through freely chosen representatives, to vote and to be elected at genuine periodic elections held on the basis of universal and equal suffrage and by secret ballot. To these formal rights must be added the political and campaign rights set out in the 1966 Covenant, which are essential to a 'meaningful election process';[1] article 19 (the right to hold opinions without interference, and to freedom of expression); article 21 (the right of peaceful assembly); and article 22 (the right to freedom of association). Considered together with the collective entitlement to free and fair elections, these provide the legal basis for a claim to representative government, but still offer an incomplete *practical* framework for effective implementation of international obligations.

The UN Human Rights Committee's General Comment on article 25, for example, highlights the areas in which guidance is still required by repeatedly invoking the standard of 'reasonableness' as a justification for conditions or restrictions on political rights, whether in the matter of voting, candidature, conflict of interest, election expenditure, or constituency delimitation.[2]

Free and fair elections as an integral element of established democracies or as a process on the way to democratization are not to be judged by what happens on polling day alone. Assessments must go beyond matters of law and form, to examine political society at large, including the nature of the electoral system, voter entitlement, voter registration, party organization, party financing, candidate selection, electoral expenses, voter education, the conduct of election campaigns, and the effectiveness of traditional political rights. In addition, the evaluation of an election as free and fair/not free and fair requires that the field of choice be examined to see whether it offers a sufficiently equitable range of opportunity among those competing for public office; whether any party or group has been prevented or arbitrarily restricted from co-operating in pursuit of electoral goals, or from accessing the media or communicating its views; and whether the election has taken place in a

---

[1] Larry Garber and Clark Gibson, *Review of United Nations Electoral Assistance 1992-93*, (Aug. 1993), 58; cf. Franck, T., 'The Emerging Right to Democratic Governance', 86 *AJIL* 46 (1992), at 61: 'the essential preconditions for an open electoral process'.

[2] Human Rights Committee, 'General Comment adopted by the Human Rights Committee under Article 40, Paragraph 4, of the International Covenant on Civil and Political Rights', Addendum, 'General Comment No. 25 (57)': UN doc. CCPR/C/21/Rev.1/Add.7, 27 Aug. 1996, paras. 4, 10, 15-17, 19-21.

generally secure environment, so that the electorate also has been able to vote without fear or intimidation, in secret, and with confidence in the system at large.

Whether rules have been violated will provide one indicator of conformity or non-conformity with international obligations. Other situations, however, involve elements of appreciation, and the question is how to determine the range of permissible variation from the norm. So far as international law is concerned with *results*, rather than with 'technical' infringements, a Code of Conduct can provide the necessary non-binding standards by which acts and actors can be judged. Not all Codes are of this nature, however, for some indeed are 'legislated', for example, by the Electoral Commission acting under statute; in such cases, their binding quality depends less on agreement between the parties and more on their legal provenance.[3]

Codes of Conduct *agreed* between the parties to an election have been increasingly accepted in a number of potentially tense situations. They have often served as a practical basis for contributing to peaceful voting, and have also helped to develop confidence in the democratic process as a mechanism for implementing representative government and effecting peaceful change. In one, somewhat unique case, adherence to a Code of Conduct was actually a condition for participation in the elections,[4] while the Code itself laid down basic campaign freedoms for all parties, underlined the prohibition of intimidation and violence at political meetings, and, in particular, established both the requirement and the modalities for regular communication between the parties.

In the Declaration on Criteria for Free and Fair Elections adopted unanimously at its March 1994 session in Paris, the Inter-Parliamentary Council urged States to take the necessary policy and institutional steps to ensure the progressive achievement and consolidation of democratic goals. Taking practical experience into account, it recommended that States should 'Encourage parties, candidates and the media to accept and adopt a Code of Conduct to govern the election campaign and the polling period'.[5]

---

[3] The author is grateful to Didier Maus for clarifying this point of distinction.

[4] See art. 7, Elections Annex to the *Comprehensive Settlement Agreement* for Cambodia 31 *ILM* 180 (1992). For further examples of Codes of Conduct, see the Annexes below.

[5] Declaration on Criteria for Free and Fair Elections, Inter-Parliamentary Council, 154th session, Paris, 26 March 1994; text in Goodwin-Gill, G. S., *Free and Fair Elections: International Law and Practice*, Inter-Parliamentary Union, Geneva, 1994, x.

1.2 Purposes of a Code of Conduct for Elections

> '... States should take the necessary policy and institutional steps to ensure the progressive achievement and consolidation of democratic goals, including through the establishment of a neutral, impartial or balanced mechanism for the management of elections. In so doing, they should, among other matters... Encourage parties, candidates and the media to accept and adopt a Code of Conduct to govern the election campaign and the polling period...'
> *Declaration on Criteria for Free and Fair Elections*, 4(2)

Codes of Conduct can contribute to fairness and to the appearance of fairness in the administration of an election. Codes supplement *rules*, but can also provide what has been called in another context, 'light touch regulatory styles that do not stress commands'.[6] The provisions of any code will necessarily depend upon the particular political and social context, and on the needs that must be met; in general, however, a code's content will be determined by reference to whether it furthers an acceptable result in terms of the criteria for free and fair elections.

In brief, a Code of Conduct can be viewed as a tool which contributes to *freedom* and *fairness*; to *effective* choice; to a *representative* and *credible* process; to *transparency* and *accountability*; to *inclusive* practices; to reducing *adversarial* relationships; and to the emergence and consolidation of a *democratic political culture*.[7] If it is effective, a Code of Conduct will promote consultation and discussion across party lines, in the interests of a 'good' election,[8] but also more generally in promoting confidence among the participants and expectations within the electorate.

The rules relating to the conduct of free and fair elections may be implemented effectively, supplemented, and fulfilled through the practical medium of a Code of Conduct. It is sometimes said that rules can go far to ensure that an election is 'free', but that a Code of Conduct is essential to guarantee and maintain that it is 'fair'. In practice, there is considerable

---

[6] Baldwin, R., *Rules and Government,* Clarendon Press, Oxford, 1995, 159.

[7] As former UN Secretary-General Boutros Boutros-Ghali noted recently, 'Support for a culture of democracy... has proved central to ensuring that electoral results are respected and that there is widespread support among all actors for the continued practice of democratic politics beyond a first referendum or election': United Nations Secretary-General, 'Support by the United Nations System of the Efforts of Governments to Promote and Consolidate New or Restored Democracies': UN doc. A/51/761, 20 Dec. 1996, para. 43.

[8] Of course, other advantages may also accrue to the process of democratization; as has been noted in general, 'Democratic institutions and processes channel competing interests into arenas of discourse and provide means of compromise which can be respected by all participants in debates, thereby minimizing the risk that differences or disputes will erupt into armed conflict or confrontation': Secretary-General, UN doc. A/51/761, above note 7, para. 17.

overlap between the two regulatory options in the pursuit of the same goal. In some situations, the role of law is clear, for example, in the prohibition of violence or incitement; a Code can reiterate the relevant rules but may also go further, indicating the sorts of conduct to be discouraged, promoting a climate of tolerance and co-operation, and encouraging issues-, not personalities-related campaigning.[9]

1.3 Codes of Conduct and the promotion of 'peaceful elections'

Though much may be hoped for in the way of self-regulation in an atmosphere of confidence and mutual trust, no law and no code is self-applying. Hence, the necessity for a mechanism of compliance, which may be an impartial and independent body, such as an Electoral Commission, or other institution accepted by the parties. A code, by definition, comprises a body of *principle,* intended for the *guidance* of those participating in an election. As likely as not its language will be ambiguous, or appear to fall short of eventualities. Reasonable people acting in good faith may misinterpret its terms, although the tension and emotions of an election also frequently lead parties and candidates to 'push the envelope' in search of every possible advantage. In some cases, penalties may be called for;[10] in others, the parties may respond positively to advisory opinions.

The 1996 elections in India showed how an active, independent election commission can revive standards through the active enforcement of both electoral laws and a code of conduct. Unlike previous elections, the 1996 Lok Sabha elections in India were remarkable for the complete absence of wall paintings, banners, posters and loudspeakers. The Election Commission fielded batteries of video camera operators to check on and record the conduct of meetings,[11] while the parties themselves were obliged to engage to a much greater extent in door-to-door campaigning.[12]

In many other instances, an election commission or equivalent body has played an important role, not so much in formal dispute settlement, as in the

---

[9]   The Pakistan Code adopted for the 1997 elections, for example, reproduces in straightforward language many of the offences laid down in the Representation of the People Act, but also provides examples of conduct to be avoided, such as calling a candidate 'traitor'; see below, Annex 3.

[10]   See further below, section 2.5

[11]   *Times of India* News Service, 11 Apr. 1996. The Election Commission also banned the showing of films featuring actors with political connections, while its activities in other areas, such as banning the export of cotton on the ground that it might influence voters in cotton-growing regions, attracted criticism for excessive zeal: *Times of India* News Service, 12, 18 Apr. 1996,

[12]   *Times of India* News Service, 17 Apr. 1996.

avoidance of disputes by requiring or facilitating regular meetings between the parties. Indeed, one criterion by which to judge electoral institutions overall is the extent to which they contribute to 'solutions', that is, not only to an efficient and effective electoral process, but to the acceptance of and belief in the process as appropriate for the selection of parliament and government in a particular culture. In this sense, the need for 'peaceful' settlement of disputes would seem ideally to require consensus (on both the process and the results), rather than 'confrontation' — that is, there will likely always be problems with a dispute resolution system that relies too much, or too obviously, on the normal mechanisms for dispute resolution in society (courts, rulings, sanctions, enforcement). In this context, 'peaceful' is something more than reaching a conclusion quickly and efficiently, but also involves building or confirming confidence in the system overall.

This in turn leads to the question of the nature of an electoral dispute, and how it compares and contrasts with any other 'civil' dispute. Although rights and duties may be involved, resolution of differences may be better framed in other language, and a 'rights' approach may not be the best basis for classification. It is important that electoral dispute resolution structures be based on at least one premise and one objective, namely, independence and impartiality; and a pro-active role for resolution or avoidance of disagreement, in certain situations at least, in order to avoid confrontation. A code of conduct, particularly where it serves to bring parties, candidates and administrators into regular contact, has certain advantages in regard to the objective in question.

2. PRACTICE AND PROBLEMS

2.1 Elections and finance

> 'States should take the necessary legislative steps and other measures, in accordance with their constitutional processes, to guarantee the rights and institutional framework for periodic and genuine, free and fair elections, in accordance with their obligations under international law. In particular, States should... Provide for the formation and free functioning of political parties, possibly regulate the funding of political parties and electoral campaigns, ensure the separation of party and State, and establish the conditions for competition in legislative elections on an equitable basis...'
> *Declaration on Criteria for Free and Fair Elections,* 4(1)
> 'States should take all necessary and appropriate measures to ensure the transparency of the entire electoral process...' *Declaration on Criteria for Free and Fair Elections,* 4(7)

In the developing world, or in situations of transition from one-party to multi-party systems, campaign financing and the public financing of political parties are generally seen as *enabling* measures, intended to go some way at least to opening the path to electoral involvement, and/or to establish or restore a measure of balance to the competition ('levelling the playing field').[13] In some developed democracies, on the other hand, private contributions, particularly from corporations or trade unions, are seen as a potential threat to the democratic process, being too often oriented to a particular legislative or political agenda. The use of public funds in support of political parties and to meet election costs, with or without controlled private financing, may then be used, but with essentially the same objective, namely, ensuring a more or less equitable balance between competing actors.

Recent experience in the USA shows what can happen where controls are meagre, unenforced or unenforceable. Then, the medium replaces the message, and candidates themselves may be marginalized by unknown advertising forces purportedly acting in their interest. Money (and what money can buy in terms of airtime, telephone canvassing, and the like), replaces public debate and the forum. When the sources of such financing are unknown and more or less untraceable, the challenge to democratic process is the more acute.

---

[13] Cf. Merloe, P., 'Electoral Campaigns and Pre-Election Issues: The "Level Playing Field" and Democratic Elections', National Democratic Institute, Washington, D.C., 1994.

That finance in its various forms can upset the equilibrium of the electoral process, even to the point of undermining the principle of self-determination, has been consistently recognized by the United Nations General Assembly over the past years. Thus, in the context of the Charter obligation 'to respect the right of others to self-determination and to determine freely their political status and pursue their economic, social and cultural development', the General Assembly in 1995 reaffirmed that,

> any activities that attempt, directly or indirectly, to interfere in the free development of national electoral processes, in particular in the developing countries, or that are intended to sway the results of such processes, violate the spirit and letter of the principles established in the Charter and in the Declaration on Principles of International Law concerning Friendly Relations and Cooperation among States in accordance with the Charter of the United Nations...

In addition, it 'strongly appealed' to 'all States to refrain from financing or providing, directly or indirectly, any other form of overt or covert support for political parties or groups and from taking actions to undermine the electoral processes in any country'.[14]

Economic and social conditions can clearly strengthen or weaken support for the democratic process, and may also bear directly on the level of ethnic or inter-communal tensions.[15] Not surprisingly, therefore, organizations such as the OSCE have stressed the importance for reforming countries of reaching agreement on 'the goals, methods and pace of economic and political initiatives through the use of democratic institutions'.[16] Recognizing, too, the importance of pluralism in regard to political organizations, the right to associate to these ends is repeatedly emphasised, as are the requisite legal guarantees 'to enable them to compete with each other on a basis of equal treatment before the law and by the authorities'.[17] That effective opportunities to participate in the political process also depend on financial considerations is implicitly acknowledged, even if the inherent problems are only hinted at in simple statements, such that 'The financing of political parties must be transparent'; or that each State should ensure that no 'legal or administrative

---

[14] UNGA res. 50/172, 'Respect for the principles of national sovereignty and non-interference in the internal affairs of States in their electoral processes,' 22 Dec. 1995, paras. 3, 5, 7.

[15] Cf. OSCE Parliamentary Assembly, Stockholm Declaration, 9 July 1996, Ch. 3 (Democracy, Human Rights and Humanitarian Questions), para. 71.

[16] Ibid., Ch. 2 (Economic Affairs, Science, Technology and Environment), paras. 38, 50.

[17] Para. 16, 'Code of Conduct on Politico-Democratic Aspects of Co-operation', approved by the OSCE Parliamentary Assembly, Stockholm, 9 July 1996; referred to the Ministerial Council and to the OSCE Lisbon Summit, December 1996, and recommended for adoption.

obstacles' impede 'access to the media on a non-discriminatory basis for all political groupings and individuals wishing to participate'.[18]

2.1.1 Financing: Some dimensions to the funding question

Given the many variations of political organization among actual and emergent democratic nations, it may be difficult to move beyond agreement on the very general principle that financing systems should be 'transparent', or that unspecified 'checks and balances' are called for, though they will likely be very much the product of particular political cultures.

To a certain extent, each political community must answer for itself what is the purpose or aim of funding political parties, as opposed to 'political life' (including civic education) in general. Some assumptions about private sector or corporate funding may also be culturally specific, and such funding is by no means always linked to the expectation of a direct advantage.[19] Funding is especially important at times of transition from single-party to multi-party systems, where it is essential to redress the balance between opposition groups and those which had long held the reins of power, in order that voters should be better informed of the issues and therefore better able to make choices.[20] The International Crisis Group, reviewing electioneering in Republika Srpska in August 1996, noted that with the injection of some 600,000 DM from the OSCE for each opposition coalition, money itself was no longer a great obstacle to the political campaign. But money alone would not overcome the problem of access to the most important media or a generally hostile communications environment.[21] With regard to the March 1996 Zimbabwe presidential elections, on the other hand, government campaign funds were reportedly denied under the constitution to any but the incumbent president's party,[22] while late payment of subsidies was claimed in both Tanzania and Haiti.[23]

The variety of problems in this area also tends to make it less suitable for the universal adoption of a set of rules. Over-regulation, indeed, may well simply lead corporations, trade unions and interest groups to divert their

---

[18] Paras. 16, 33, 'Code of Conduct for Politico-Democratic Aspects of Co-operation', annexed to the July 1996 Stockholm Declaration, above note 17.

[19] But see below, on recent experience in the United States of America.

[20] See *Free and Fair Elections,* 58-61.

[21] International Crisis Group Bosnia Project, 'Electioneering in Republika Srpska', Aug. 1996.

[22] Rotberg, Robert I, 'Democracy in Africa: The Ballot doesn't Tell All', *Christian Science Monitor,* 1 May 1996.

[23] Commonwealth Observer Group, *The Union Presidential and Parliamentary Elections in Tanzania, 29 October 1995,* (1996), 15; OAS/Unit for the Promotion of Democracy, 'Establishment of the Electoral Observer Mission of the Organization of American States', Nov. 1995.

political contributions to parties and candidates into research institutes and 'action committees' beyond the area of possible control.

Practice in some jurisdictions nevertheless illuminates concerns and responses.[24] Subsidies for campaign expenses, for example, may be conditional on filing periodic statements of income, assets and expenditure; tax credits may be available for political contributions, generally within limits; certain types of contributions may be prohibited, sometimes by reference to source;[25] overall expenditures may be capped; and all contributions or contributions over a prescribed amount may require to be disclosed.[26] Thus, Belgian law prohibits all contributions from corporations or trade unions, and provides that those from individuals should *not* be tax deductible.[27] In Canada, there are no restrictions on the amount that may be received by the candidate's official agent, but no one and no registered party may receive or use contributions from a person who is not a Canadian citizen or permanent resident, a corporation or association that does not carry on business in Canada, a trade union that does not hold bargaining rights for employees in Canada, any foreign political party, or a foreign government or agent of a foreign government. It is also illegal to make contributions to anyone but the official agent, all donations over $100 must be disclosed, anonymous contributions under $100 must be identified as to category (for example, individual or corporate), and 'anonymous' contributions over $100 must either be identified by reference to amount, name and category, or the money sent to the Receiver General of Canada through Elections Canada.[28] Individual donations continue to make up the bulk of contributions.[29]

---

[24]   Information following on European practice draws in part on Council of Europe, 'Financing of Political Parties: Legislation' (1994), a collection compiled for the use of the Council of Europe Project Group, 'Human Rights and Genuine Democracy' and related meetings, including the European Workshop on the Financing of Political Parties, Turku/Åbo, Finland, 17-18 May 1995.

[25]   In the United States, the following are among those prohibited: contributions from non-citizens or non-permanent residents; contributions in another's name; cash contributions in excess of $100; direct contributions to candidates from corporations or trade unions. Many allegations regarding finance and campaign funding surfaced in the aftermath of the 1996 US elections; these included claims that both the Democratic and the Republican parties raised a considerable amount of 'soft money', that is, non-accountable contributions, and that both parties relied heavily on indirect and again non-accountable promotional activities by various groups. A number of lawsuits were initiated, for example, against the largest teachers' union in Washington state, claiming that it had illegally spent teachers' dues on political campaigns and failed to report campaign activity: *Seattle Times,* 12 Feb. 1997.

[26]   Cf. Mandate of the Ontario Commission on Election Finances, Canada; Election Finances Act; Municipal Elections Act.

[27]   Loi du 4 juillet 1989 'relative à la limitation et au contrôle des dépenses électorales ainsi qu'au financement et a la comptabilité ouverte des partis politiques': *Moniteur belge,* 20 juillet 1989, 206. The French law of 1995 also prohibits contributions by corporations and limits individual contributions to 50,000F; donations over 1,000F must be made by cheque: see Camby, Jean-Pierre, *Le financement de la vie politique en France,* (1995), 55-9.

[28]   Elections Canada, Election Handbook for Candidates, their Official Agents and Auditors, Ottawa, 1993.

[29]   The 2,156 candidates who filed nomination papers received 160,944 contributions totalling $42,210,219. Individuals constituted the majority of donors, both in number and amount, totalling 131,245 individual contributions to candidates = $17,565,542 = 41.6 per cent. Next, businesses and commercial corporations (23.4%), political organizations such as local associations (18.7%), and registered political parties (11.6%): Elections Canada, Contributions and Expenses of Registered Political Parties and Candidates, 35th General Election 1993, Ottawa, 1993. See also Seidle, F. Leslie, ed., *Issues in Party and Election Finance in Canada,* Research Studies of the Royal Commission on Electoral Reform and Party Financing, 5, Toronto, Dundurn Press, 1991.

Elsewhere, public funding may be tied to *effort*, for example, by matching State subsidies to party recruitment. In the highly regulated United States system, donors can contribute cash to parties and candidates, but donations are not allowed by corporations, trade unions, national banks and foreign nationals.[30] They may set up 'political action committees', however, which can serve as a channel for donations to candidates.[31]

In Austria, the principle of government funding dates from 1975; contributions consist of a fixed sum equal to about 3 million Austrian schillings for all political parties having at least 5 representatives in Parliament, plus a variable reflecting the overall standing of the parties, by reference to the number of votes received during the previous election.[32] In 1989, a further contribution to election costs was introduced, calculated by reference to votes received and representation in Parliament, and additional funding may be available for so-called 'parliamentary clubs' of parties competing in an election, and for political education and journalism.

In Belgium, the 1989 law on electoral expenses, party financing and accountability defines income and expenditure, lays down the maximum that can be spent during legislative and provincial elections, and determines the basis for calculating the annual subsidy for every party represented in the House and the Senate by at least one member, which must be paid to the non-profit institution designated by the party.[33]

The 1990 Bulgarian law on political parties prescribes permissible sources of funding: initial and membership dues; donations and legacies; income from business activity; and State subsidies. It also prohibits certain types of contribution, including donations that are anonymous, or from foreign States and organizations, or from institutions, enterprises or organizations. State funding for elections and political activities is determined by reference to numbers in Parliament.

---

[30] See generally Cantor, Joseph E., Congressional Research Service (CRS) Report for Congress, 'Campaign Financing in Federal Elections: A Guide to the Law and its Operation,' 8 Aug. 1986; updated 15 Oct. 1993.

[31] Individuals may contribute a maximum of $1,000 to each candidate, and $20,000 to a national party per election; political action committees (PACs), $5,000 and $15,000, respectively. For brief discussion of the contributions and influence of PACs, see, among others, Cantor, 'Campaign Financing in Federal Elections', above note 30, 31-2; Kalb, D. & Salant, J.D., 'Donations by Pro-Israel PACs in Decline on Capitol Hill', *Congressional Quarterly*, 16 Mar. 1996, 719; '1995 Campaign Finance Totals', ibid., 6 Apr. 1996, 954; Salant, J., 'Freshmen Embrace Capitol Ways as They Go for PAC Donations', ibid., 20 Apr. 1996, 1068; also Weiser, Benjamin & McAllister, Bill, 'The Little Agency That Can't. Election-Law Enforcer is Weak by Design, Paralyzed by Division', *Washington Post*, 12 Feb. 1997.

[32] 'Bundesgesetz vom 2. Juli 1975 über die Aufgaben, Finanzierung und Wahlverbung politischer Parteien (Parteingestetz)', art. II.

[33] Loi du 4 juillet 1989 'relative à la limitation et au contrôle des dépenses électorales ainsi qu'au financement et à la comptabilité ouverte des partis politiques': *Moniteur belge*, 20 juillet 1989, 206, arts. 4, 16, 22.

The Danish Parliament enacted the Grants to Political Parties, etc. Act in 1986, which provides for grants to both political parties and independent candidates, on the basis of five Danish kroner per vote per year for general elections.[34] Historically, the trade unions had traditionally provided financial support to the social democratic party, while business interests were the source for the so-called bourgeois parties. This effectively allowed only limited opportunities for other parties, putting in question the equity of the situation between the few with stable financing and all the others; to this were added problems of principle, and objections to funding political activity out of mandatory union dues, regardless of individual wishes. The decrease in party membership during the 1950s and 1960s helped the introduction of the public support scheme, although as some commentators have noted, this in turn allowed in a measure of public control.[35] Moreover, it is suggested that the Danish scheme is 'neutral' only in the sense that it preserves existing differences, being based on representation and votes received.[36]

Hungarian law provides for subsidies to parties represented in Parliament and according to votes received. It further lays down that, apart from such subsidy, no party may accept a contribution from the State, or from another State; and that all anonymous donations must be paid to a public interest foundation. There are sanctions for non-compliance; illegal contributions must be surrendered to the State, while a party at fault may lose its subsidy up to the amount of the illegal contribution.[37]

Portugal employs a combination of public and private funding, with the former including grants to finance parties and electoral campaigns, as well as subsidies granted by the European Parliament under European Community law.[38] Spain's 1987 law likewise covers both public and private sources. Public financing to pay electoral expenses is granted on the basis of the number of votes and members of Parliament obtained in the election by each party; parliamentary groups in the Congress and Senate, and in regional

---

[34] See Pedersen, M.N. and Bille, 'Public Financing and Public Control of Political Parties in Denmark', in Wiberg, Matti, *The Public Purse and Political Parties. Political Financing of Political Parties in Nordic Countries.* Finnish Political Science Association. 1991, 147-72. The authors noted incidentally that initially 'parties were considered anathema in the Danish parliament during the first decades of the democratic era...The first democratic constitution — of 1849 — had proclaimed that "members of parliament are solely expected to follow their own conscience and are not bound by any directions by their voters".' (148)

[35] Ibid., 166.

[36] Ibid.

[37] Law XXXIII (1989) on political parties, as amended by Law LXII (1990), Law XLIV (1991) and Law LXXI (1992).

[38] Law 72/93, 30 Nov. 1993; Law 77/88, 1 Jul. 1988; Regional Legislative Decree 9/86/A, 20 Mar. 1986 (Azores); Regional Legislative Decree 24/89/M, 7 Sept. 1989 (Madeira).

chambers also receive funding, while yearly subsidies go to parties with members in the national Congress, according to the number of votes and members of that Chamber obtained in the previous election.[39] Private funding comprises membership fees, contributions (subject to limits and conditions), legacies, returns on capital and credits.[40]

Sweden's Act 1972:625 on Financial Assistance to Political Parties provides for payments to be made to each party that has obtained a significant number of votes over two elections, and to unrepresented parties that have obtained more than 2.5 per cent of votes cast in the latest election. Provision is also made for office assistance and various other contributions.

A 1988 report commission by the Swiss parliament noted that political parties were in a difficult situation, and that they faced new challenges from 'les associations d'intérêts, les médias et d'autres formes nouvelles d'action politique'.[41] With a view to *promoting* the parties, it also called attention to the dangers inherent in inequality of opportunity, for example, where party independence is replaced by dependence on a few generous donors. It identified three guiding principles for State support of political parties in a democratic system:[42] 'la démocratie politique', in which parties occupy a critical juncture between citizens and the organs of the State, and which ought not to be compromised by even the appearance of common interest between party and State; 'la liberté des partis', a fundamental right flowing from freedom of association in general and which includes freedom of creation and freedom of action; and 'l'égalité des partis', which presupposes equality of support by the State and contains the kernel of the problem, for should State aid support and promote formal equality, material equality, or equality of opportunity?

A recent study on the United Kingdom concluded that, 'the legal limitation of election expenses under the Corrupt Practices Act of 1883 and its successors has been a spectacular success: candidates are able to stand and campaign for election without the need for substantial financial resources, and the rules have been by and large observed.'[43] Political parties are privately financed, and no restrictions other than the general law govern how money is raised. At a general election, the candidate appoints an agent who is responsible in law for all expenses incurred in the candidate's constituency

---

[39] See Basic Law 3/87; Basic Law 5/85.

[40] Basic Law 9/91 creates the crime of influence peddling, and is intended to ensure that private contributions to political parties are not made in consideration for favours relating to public activity.

[41] Conseil fédéral, 'Rapport sur l'aide aux partis politiques', 23 nov. 1988 (doc. 88.075).

[42] Ibid., §§35, 351-3.

[43] *Agenda for Change*. The Report of the Hansard Society Commission on Election Campaigns. Hansard Society, London, 1991, 35.

campaign. Candidates are limited in what they may spend, comprising a basic amount plus so much per eligible registered voter.[44] Political parties, however, can spend without limits, provided it is not in support of a particular candidate, and this is giving rise to increasing concern.[45] No financial assistance as such is provided for electoral expenses, but the parties receive fairly significant assistance in kind, including free broadcasting time, free use of halls for election meetings, free postal delivery to every elector.[46]

In the Federal Republic of Germany, all candidates are funded by political parties, which in turn receive more than 60 per cent of campaign funds from the government; corporate donations are permitted (but are not tax deductible) and, within certain limits, contributions need not be disclosed. Individuals also are a source of membership fees and donations, which are tax deductible now only to DM 6,000.[47] The Russian Presidential Election Law 1995 restricted legal funding to those funds allocated to a candidate for the pre-election campaign by the Central Election Commission; the candidate's own funds, not exceeding some $11,000; and other funds, also with varying limits, including those allocated to the candidate by the electoral association or nominating group; and voluntary donations by individuals and legal entities. The ceiling of total campaign expenditures was set at approximately $2.87 million.[48]

Several commentators consider that large and anonymous donations enhance the possibility of corruption, and should therefore be declared. Small and individual contributions, on the other hand, should be as entitled to anonymity (as a reflection of the individual right to privacy) as the exercise of

---

[44]   Section 75(1), Representation of the People Act 1983: 'No expenses shall, with a view to promoting or procuring the election of a candidate and an election, be incurred by any person other than the candidate, his election agent and persons authorised in writing by the election agent'.

[45]   The Report of the Hansard Society Commission on Election Campaigns, *Agenda for Change,* Hansard Society, London, 1991, 37-9, noted that such advertising was 'widely believed to be efficacious, giving an advantage to whichever party can afford to spend most', and that there was considerable public support for spending limits.

[46]   The Hansard Society Report noted that, on balance, public opinion was against the public subsidy of campaign costs: above note 45, 46.

[47]   'Sechstes Gesetz zur Änderung des Parteiengesetzes und anderer Gesetze vom 28. Januar 1994': 1 *BGBl.* 1994, 142. Under art. 18, a global limit is set, out of which no single party may receive more than it earned during the year. The assessment of the subsidy is made by reference to the parties receiving a threshold of votes cast, and is based on DM 1 for every vote cast, plus DM 0.5 for every DM 1.0 obtained as fee or donation (by an individual up to DM 6,000), plus a further DM 0.30 for every valid vote cast up to 5 million.

[48]   OSCE, 'Report on the Election of the President of the Russian Federation, 16 June and 3 July 1996', 9-10. Candidate and campaign expenses were expressed in terms of so many minimum monthly salaries; for example, voluntary donations by individuals were not to exceed 50 minimum monthly salaries (approximately $11.36). It was claimed that the overall limits were exceeded by the incumbent president, and the OSCE delegation also noted that the linkage of the presidential campaign with that of Moscow's mayor 'may have been a creative way of circumventing campaign finance limitations'. It recommended that the Central Electoral Commission monitor and enforce compliance with financial rules, and that the cap on expenditures apply to all candidates. See also IFES, *Europe and Asia Report,* Feb. 1997, 7, reporting with regard to the 1995 and 1996 elections in Russia, that 'vast monetary resources actually spent on campaigns are unaccounted for', that 'widely varying sums are publicly cited', but that 'the only common feature about these sums is that they fail to correspond in any way to the figures provided in official reports.'

the right to vote itself. The most important consideration in this context appears to be *transparency;* corporations, in particular, should disclose their contributions, and political parties, their income.

2.1.2 Financing and Code of Conduct issues

The extent to which election-related contributions and expenditures admit of regulation will clearly depend on a variety of factors in each country's particular legal and political culture. In the United States, the otherwise high level of control has been upset by the general unwillingness of the parties to limit fund-raising and expenditure, and by the impact of the constitutional protection accorded to free speech.[49] The unwillingness to submit to control is reflected institutionally in the Federal Election Commission (FEC), the agency established by Congress to regulate the financial side to the electoral process. The FEC, with representation evenly divided between both political parties, is easily blocked by divisions along party lines, while its opportunities for independent action are severely limited.[50] Nevertheless, the 1996 elections generated new moves to reform campaign finance, with proposals for both mandatory and voluntary limits, and with incentives for compliance attaching to the latter.[51]

In India also all party discussions in mid-1996 focused on compulsory account-keeping by political parties, audits under the authority of the Election Commission, and a ban on corporate donations to parties; the question of State funding, however, proved more contentious.[52] The rational justification for limitations nevertheless reveals certain perceptions common across the democratic spectrum.

With regard to the Canadian approach, for example, it has been said that,

Fairness requires that access for paid partisan messages in the media be restricted in order to limit the cost of election campaigns. General restrictions on spending during election campaigns are legitimate and necessary in order to ensure equality of opportunity among candidates and among registered political parties. The provision of partial

---

[49]   Cf. Axworthy, T., 'Capital Intensive Politics', in Seidle, Leslie F., *Issues in Party and Election Finance in Canada,'* above note 29, who remarks that while limiting expenditures may intrude on liberty, unlimited spending makes a mockery of equality. He also considers that Canadian law does not go far enough, for example, in counteracting the influence of government and interest groups.

[50]   See Weiser & McAllister, *Washington Post* above note 31. The FEC is unable to launch criminal investigations, to impose penalties or seek injunctions before elections to bring illegal activity to an end.

[51]   Draft legislation submitted to Congress included the Campaign Finance Reform Act of 1996: H.R. 3760; the American Political Reform Act: H.R. 3505; and H.R. 2566 and S. 1219 (the Smith and McCain-Feingold bills). The last-mentioned proposals included the offer of reduced media costs as an incentive for compliance

[52]   *The Hindu,* 29 Aug. 1996.

reimbursements... and of income tax credits for political contributions help both to encourage participation... and to promote fairness...[53]

Jean-Pierre Camby has observed that the financing of parties and campaigns touches fundamental elements of the life of the political community.[54] He quotes Yves Mény:

> la démocratie, par principe, se règle sur le principe 'un homme une voix', affirme le traitement égal de tous les citoyens, récuse l'argent en tant qu'élément discriminant.[55]

The principles of equality, of equal opportunity to participate in public life, and of the equal value of each vote, are all challenged by the weight of money.[56] The French legislation of 1988, 1990 and 1995 established fixed and controlled expenditure limits and broke the inflationary spiral by forbidding purely and simply certain of the most expensive forms of propaganda.[57] It brought the electoral campaign back to essentials and the candidates into the campaign; as one commentator put it, 'Moins d'argent égale plus de qualité'.[58]

At the same time, many jurisdictions, like those in the United States, have attempted to wrestle with the impact of constitutional guarantees of democratic process. The *Conseil constitutionnel* in France, for example, struck down a provision limiting State aid to parties having obtained at least 5% of votes, 'car ce seuil était de nature à entraver l'expression de nouveaux courants d'idées et d'opinions', and therefore contrary to the combined effect of articles 2 and 4 of the Constitution, to the principle of equality and political parties' freedom of activity.[59]

---

[53] *Strengthening the Foundation,* Annex to the Report of the Chief Electoral Officer of Canada on the 35th General Election, Ottawa, 1996, 55.

[54] Camby, Jean-Pierre, *Le financement de la vie politique en France,* Montchrestien, Paris, 1995, 10.

[55] *Pouvoirs,* no. 65, p. 72.

[56] Camby also quotes Jean-Claude Masclet: 'Si tant qu'il n'existe pas de politique sans vertu, on peut convenir que la vertu passe aujourd'hui par la clarté dans la connaissance du financement de la vie politique et par des mesures qui, tel le financement public, assurent l'égalité dans la lutte des idées': 'Le prix de la démocratie', *Mélanges Gaudemet,* (1984), 120.

[57] Loi du 11 mars 1988 relative à la transparence financière de la vie politique; loi du 15 janvier 1990 relative à la limitation des dépenses électorales et à la clarification du financement des activités politiques; loi no. 95-65 du 19 janvier 1995 sur le financement de la vie politique. Cf. ODIHR, *Final Report,* Bulgarian Presidential Election, October 27 and November 3, 1996, reporting the widespread use of full-colour posters and doubting whether any major candidate could have avoided spending more than the legal limit.

[58] Millon, Charles, 'Avant/après: Ce qui a changé', in 'L'argent des élections', *Pouvoirs,* No. 70, 1994, 103, 109, 111. Also, Doublet, Yves-Marie, 'La législation de 1995 sur le financement de la vie politique', *Revue française de droit constitutionnel,* no. 22, 1995, 411.

[59] Décision No. 89-271 D.C. du 11 janvier 1990, cited by Camby, *Le financement de la vie politique en France,* 33-5.

Another frequently invoked rationale is tied to *transparency*. Noting the tendency for the media now to dominate politics, Charles Millon has remarked that, 'la clarification des relations entretenues par les élus et leur sources de financement est un problème central. La baisse de la pression de l'argent sur les hommes politiques, c'est... le premier pas vers un recentrage indispensable de leur rôle et de leurs missions'.[60] In 'Guidelines on the financing of political parties' prepared for the Council of Europe Working Group, Pierre Koenig observed that, 'In addition to the principle of freedom (of expenditure), funding is... subject to the principle of complete transparency.'[61] In an earlier study, he went further and suggested that 'the principles of transparency and equality of parties with regard to sources of funding... by definition, can only be fully guaranteed for public funding'.[62]

In the United States the emphasis on transparency is covered by the requirements of disclosure. A principal element in the legislation of the 1970s was disclosure of receipts and expenses by candidates and committees and an independent regulatory agency (the Federal Election Commission—FEC) to administer the law. All candidates and political committees in federal elections are subject to uniform disclosure requirements, under which contributions and expenditures must be reported on a regular basis for public examination.[63] The US Supreme Court has also upheld disclosure requirements on the ground that, like contribution limits, they help to combat corruption through stemming candidates' dependence on large campaign contributions.[64]

2.1.3 Money and the means of communication

Money has acquired a major importance in politics because of changes in the means of expression and communication.[65] Modern 'marketing' methods, including billboards, posters, mailings, telephone canvassing, and so forth, may bring more information to the voters, but also tend to standardize the

---

[60] Millon, Charles, 'Avant/après: Ce qui a changé', in 'L'argent des élections', *Pouvoirs*, No. 70, 1994, 103: '[Les dérives provoquées par l'explosion des besoins de financement] sont en effet profondément liées à la logique médiatique qui tend à dominer la politque'.

[61] Council of Europe, Project Group, 'Human Rights and Genuine Democracy', European Workshop on the Financing of Political Parties, Turku/Åbo, Finland, 17-18 May 1995, 'Guidelines on the financing of political parties', prepared by Pierre Koenig: CE doc. CAHDD(95)5, 7 Mar. 1995, 4.

[62] 'Funding of political parties', Study prepared by Pierre Koenig: CE doc. CAHDD(94)45, 20 Sept. 1994, 4-5. Cf. Camby, *Le financement de la vie politique en France*, 48 '... on ne peut tout à la fois interdire aux parties de recevoir certains dons, souhaiter qu'ils fonctionnent bien, que leurs comptes soient transparentes, et ne pas envisager un financement sur fonds public'.

[63] These are now available, regularly updated, on the FEC's WebSite: **www.fec.gov**

[64] *Buckley v. Valeo*, 424.11.51(1976); see below, note 69.

[65] Cf. Millon, Charles, 'Avant/après: Ce qui a changé', in 'L'argent des élections', *Pouvoirs*, No. 70, 1994, 103, 106.

debate; the result is that issues do not get discussed, the individual views of candidates are lost, and increasingly they are elected less on the basis of personality and more as spokespersons of particular parties. The spiralling media attention may be accompanied by greater passivity among voters, especially as ideologies decline. Polls, it has been suggested, are replacing the relationship between candidate and voter. All this costs money, which in turn is perceived as distorting the debate.[66]

The 1996 elections in the United States of America were dominated by expenditures on all sides, at an estimated overall cost of some $2.65 billion.[67] The strict limits on campaign contributions, adopted in the 1970s, were circumvented through the raising of so-called soft money, considered non-accountable because not used to promote or oppose particular candidates. Instead, much of it was used to finance what was known as 'issues advertising'.[68] In addition, the principle of full disclosure of campaign contributions and spending was circumvented by the activities of 'interest groups' supposedly independent of the parties and therefore not bound by the rules of accountability. The US Supreme Court also encouraged spending activity when it held that unlimited sums could be spent on congressional campaigns, provided the money went through operations independent of the candidates.[69] This in turn led to considerable 'outside' involvement in local

---

[66] Ibid.

[67] Marcus, Ruth & Babcock, Charles R., 'The System Cracks under the Weight of Cash: Candidates, Parties and Outside Interests Dropped a Record $2.7 Billion', *Washington Post,* 9 Feb. 1997. This is the first of a series of articles which also included Gugliotta, Guy & Chinoy, Ira, 'Money-Machine: The Fund-Raising Frenzy of Campaign '96. Outsiders Made Erie Battle a National Battle', *Washington Post,* 10 Feb. 1997; Pianin, Eric, 'Money-Machine: The Fund-Raising Frenzy of Campaign '96. How Business Found Benefits in Wage Bill', *Washington Post,* 11 Feb. 1997; and Weiser, Benjamin & McAllister, Bill, 'The Little Agency That Can't. Election-Law Enforcer is Weak by Design, Paralyzed by Division', *Washington Post,* 12 Feb. 1997.

[68] Individuals, corporations and trade unions may give as much 'soft money' to national parties as they want; it may not be spent directly for a candidate, but can be used for 'administrative' costs. In addition, individual and PACs may contribute unlimited sums for or against a candidate, provided the expenditure is not co-ordinated with party or candidate and is reported to the Federal Election Commission. According to Marcus & Babcock, *Washington Post* (above note 67), the Democratic National Committee, rather than the Clinton-Gore Campaign, paid for a series of pre-election issues advertisements, thereby avoiding the $36 million limit on candidates during the primaries. Because the advertisements were not intended to put forward particular candidates, the origin and amount of the cash spent by outside groups did not have to be reported to the Federal Election Commission, and did not need to be financed by the 'political action committees' which, in turn, were unable to accept more than $5,000 from individual donors. The Republican National Committee is reported to have engaged in similar activity, raising 'record amounts from the telecommunications, tobacco and pharmaceutical companies seeking relief from federal regulators': Marcus & Babcock, ibid.

[69] In *Buckley v. Valeo* 424 U.S. 1 (1976), the US Supreme Court upheld *contribution limits* and *disclosure requirements* because they served the 'vital governmental interest' of safeguarding the integrity of the electoral process without unduly burdening the rights of citizens and candidates to engage in political debate. It struck down *expenditure limits,* however, as representing an undue burden on political expression and did not sufficiently contribute to any overriding interest, such as preventing corruption or the appearance of corruption. This opened the way to unlimited campaign spending overall, as well as unlimited expenditure of personal funds by candidates and spending by individuals or groups. See generally Cantor, 'Campaign Financing in Federal Elections', above note 30; Durbin, Thomas M., CRS Report for Congress, 'First Amendment Issues and Major Supreme Court Decisions relating to Campaign Finance Law', updated 15 Sept. 1995.

electoral activities, often to the considerable surprise of the candidates themselves.[70] Campaign finances in the United States are by no means the only aspect of the money/democratic process debate. Corporate contributions have also been linked to the legislative agenda, even though a direct relationship between cash paid and votes gathered is rarely admitted.[71]

2.1.4 Preliminary conclusions

It is probably quite unrealistic to expect democratic elections to be separated entirely from the question of money. Indeed, the draft campaign finance act proposed by the Council on Governmental Ethics Laws (COGEL) opens with explicit recognition of the fact that financial contributions are a legitimate form of political participation, while nevertheless emphasizing that 'the financial strength of certain individuals or organizations should not permit them to exercise a disproportionate or controlling influence on the election of candidates'.[72] With particular reference to the United States, but also with relevance to emerging concerns in other countries,[73] the COGEL draft notes that the increasing cost of elections leads candidates to seek larger contributions from interest groups 'with a financial stake' in certain matters before government, resulting in the public perception that votes are being influenced by contributions. Moreover, the necessity for office holders to engage increasingly in fund-raising, 'distracts them from important public matters, encourages contributions that may have a corrupting influence, and gives incumbents an unfair advantage...' The intent of COGEL's model law is stated clearly: 'To ensure that individuals and interest groups have a fair and equal opportunity to participate... To reduce the influence of large contributors with a specific financial stake... To assist serious candidates in raising enough money to communicate their views and positions adequately...

---

[70] Gugliotta & Chinoy, *Washington Post* (above note 67), cite one campaign in which the individual candidates spent some $417,000 and $1.2 million respectively, and outside interests 'at least $1.4 million'. The Canada Elections Act restricts any person or group other than a candidate or the candidate's representative from incurring advertising expenses in excess of $1,000 to directly promote or oppose a particular registered political party or the election of a particular candidate; see subsections 259.1(1), 259.2(2). In *Somerville v. Attorney General of Canada* on 5 June 1996 the Court of Appeal of Alberta held that these provisions (and subsection 213(10)) prohibiting advertising during the so-called blackout period) violated the freedoms of expression and association and the right to vote and were not justified in a free and democratic society.

[71] See Pianin, *Washington Post* above note 67. On large contributions to candidates and the question of undue influence, see also Padget, D. in Seidle, Leslie F., ed., *Issues in Party and Election Finance in Canada,* above note 29; also, Ewing, Keith D., *Money, Politics and Law: A Study of Electoral Campaign Finance Reform in Canada,* Clarendon Press, Oxford, 1992; Linton, M., *Money and Votes,* Institute for Public Policy Research, London, 1994.

[72] Council on Governmental Ethics Laws (COGEL), 'A Model Law for Campaign Finance, Ethics and Lobbying Regulation, (1991).

[73] See IFES, *Europe and Asia Report,* Feb. 1997, 7, in which Russian Election Commissioner Kalushin cites concern with several issues common to many countires, including activity by groups in election campaigns that can affect the outcome, but which is not subject to finance regulation.

To limit overall expenditures... To provide a neutral source of campaign financing...'[74]

2.2 Elections and the media

'Every candidate for election and every political party shall have an equal opportunity of access to the media, particularly the mass communications media, in order to put forward their political views.' *Declaration on Criteria for Free and Fair Elections,* 3(4)

'... States should take the necessary policy and institutional steps to ensure the progressive achievement and consolidation of democratic goals... In so doing, they should, among other matters... Encourage parties, candidates and the media to accept and adopt a Code of Conduct to govern the election campaign and the polling period...' *Declaration on Criteria for Free and Fair Elections,* 4(2)

'In time of elections, the State and its organs should... ensure... [t]hat parties and candidates are free to communicate their views to the electorate, and that they enjoy equality of access to State and public-service media; That the necessary steps are taken to guarantee non-partisan coverage in State and public-service media.' *Declaration on Criteria for Free and Fair Elections,* 4(3).

'In order that elections shall be fair, States should take the necessary measures to ensure that parties and candidates enjoy reasonable opportunities to present their electoral platform.' *Declaration on Criteria for Free and Fair Elections,* 4(4)

2.2.1 Role of the media

As with most aspects of the political process, the relative importance of the various media will depend on economic, social and cultural factors. The importance of newspapers is contingent on a certain standard of literacy; that of radio or television, on the availability of receivers; roadside billboard advertising is of value only on roads much travelled by. In the 1996 Bangladesh elections, for example, radio was particularly important;[75] given an estimated 80 per cent illiteracy rate, it was also the 'communication

---

[74]   Model Law for Campaign Finance, Ethics and Lobbying Regulation, §102. Alexander, Herbert E. & Corrado, Anthony, *Financing the 1992 Election,* M.E. Sharpe, Armonk, WY, 1995; reviewed by Sharon Steward in *The Guardian* (Journal of the Council on Governmental Ethics Laws—COGEL), Mar. 1996, 1-3, suggests that the US system should consider, among others, 'floors without ceilings', which would ensure all serious contenders have a reasonable minimum level of funding without limiting how much candidates can spend.

[75]   Commonwealth Observer Group, *The Parliamentary Elections in Bangladesh, 12 June 1996,* Commonwealth Secretariat, London, 1997, 12-16.

medium of primary importance' in Sierra Leone,[76] although the media's direct role was ultimately minimal; this 'created an information vacuum in the country... (and) had a deleterious effect on the nature of political discourse.'[77] In assessing the Tanzanian elections in 1995, the Commonwealth Observer Group remarked that the media's role included giving people 'the means to make their choice an informed one, thus enabling them to fully participate in the democratic process'.[78] Although private newspapers and radio had been established in 1992, most people in rural areas continued to rely on state-owned radio, estimated to be 'the source of about 90 per cent of news for Tanzanians'. None of the private radio stations could match its reach, while mainland newspaper circulation and television reception were restricted to coastal areas.

In the Bosnia and Herzegovina elections in 1996, on the other hand, an opinion poll showed that 46 per cent of people in Bosniac-controlled Federation territory considered television as their principal source of information, and 'the influence of state television was even more pervasive' in Republika Srpska and Croat-controlled territory, given the absence there of alternative media.[79] Not surprisingly, the OSCE Regulations concerning the Obligations of Governments in Relation to the Media in Bosnia and Herzegovina referred to journalism as 'an important service to the public', and obliged governments not to 'impose any sanctions or penalties on journalists, nor subject them to detention, harassment or interference of any kind, in pursuit of their legitimate professional activities'.[80]

Television was also perceived as the 'key medium' in the Armenian presidential election in 1996, 'due to limited circulation of the print media and the relatively small funds available for each candidate to have equal access to free advertising on State TV and Radio.' The OSCE Office for Democratic Institutions and Human Rights regretted, however, that the media were otherwise less active than others in monitoring the election process.[81]

---

[76] Commonwealth Observer Group, *The Presidential and Parliamentary Elections in Sierra Leone, 26-27 February 1996*, Commonwealth Secretariat, London, 1996, 16. However, the Group also noted that both print and electronic media had become 'weak and emasculated' in the last years of authoritarianism.

[77] Ibid., 32. 'In the absence of reliable information the country was rampant with rumour. Perceptions based on little or no hard evidence quickly became accepted as fact... If Sierra Leone's new democracy is to succeed, it must be given political content. (T)he people...need to direct their new assertiveness into a constructive discourse about the future of their country. For that they need a revitalised media through which a vigorous public debate can take place.' The events of June 1997 appear to have justified these residual doubts about the strength of local democratic institutions and culture.

[78] Commonwealth Observer Group, *The Union Presidential and Parliamentary Elections in Tanzania, 29 October 1995*, Commonwealth Secretariat, London, 1996, 17-18.

[79] International Crisis Group, 'Elections in Bosnia and Herzegovina', ICG Report, 22 Sept. 1996, 19-24.

[80] Art. 126, Regulations Concerning the Obligations of Governments in Relation to the Media in Bosnia and Herzegovina. See also below, Annexe 1: Code of Conduct for Elections in the Region under limited Nations Transitional Administration in Eastern Slavonia, Baranja and Western Sirmium (UNTAES), Part III.

[81] OSCE, Office for Democratic Institutions and Human Rights, 'Final Report. Armenian Presidential Election, September 22, 1996'.

Besides providing news, the media have an obvious, but not always developed, role in civic education. The OAS Electoral Observation Mission to Haiti in 1995 regretted that more had not been done in the way of timely communication, information and explanation, which could have helped to lower tension.[82] The Lusaka Protocol for peace in Angola similarly acknowledged 'the importance of the mass media sector for improving the climate of tolerance and mutual trust' necessary for national reconciliation; the right of access to State press, radio and television was therefore guaranteed to political parties.[83]

2.2.2 Access to the media

Rules can go a long way towards ensuring the access of political parties to certain media, such as public-owned radio and television broadcasting services, and can require that the printed media are opened to political messages.[84] In the United States, statutory sanctions apply to broadcasters in certain circumstances. For example, a station licence may be revoked in the case of 'willful or repeated failure to allow reasonable access to or to permit purchase of reasonable amounts of time for the use of a broadcasting station by a legally qualified candidate for Federal elective office on behalf of his candidacy'.[85] Likewise, any licensee who allows a candidate for public office to use a broadcasting station, is required to afford 'equal opportunities to all other (legally qualified) candidates'. There is no obligation, however, to allow use overall, although there is an obligation, in connection with news broadcasts and the like, 'to operate in the public interest and to afford reasonable opportunity for the discussion of conflicting views on issues of public importance.'[86]

French law makes a distinct difference between access to audiovisual media and access to printed media. Audiovisual media in the public domain are required to disseminate political broadcasts on the basis of strict equality, although with questionable distinctions between parties represented in the National Assembly and others who may nevertheless be fielding a significant number of candidates. The *Conseil supérieur de l'audiovisuel* may make

---

[82] Final Report of the OAS Electoral Observation Mission to the Legislative and Municipal Elections in Haiti (1995), s. 3.7.

[83] Lusaka Protocol, Annex 6, Agenda Item II.4: National Reconciliation, Pt. II, 3.

[84] 'Access', of course, brings other issues in its wake, including questions of allocation and cost.

[85] 47 U.S.C. §312(7). Cf. the provision in United Kingdom law, which restricts broadcast coverage of *constituency* campaigns without the consent of *all* individual candidates: section 93, Representation of the People Act. Intended to prevent one candidate from gaining a media advantage, this provision effectively allows a veto and also prevents coverage of groups or categories of candidates, such as women or ethnic minorities. Its repeal was recommended by the Hansard Society Commission on Election Campaigns: *Agenda for Change,* 52.

[86] 47 U.S.C. §315(a)

recommendations to the privately-owned media, reminding them of the applicable rules of equal treatment. With regard to print media, however, the *Conseil constitutionnel* has always maintained that the principle of freedom of the press forbids the imposition of the principle of equal access.[87]

Notwithstanding the role for rules, reports of recent elections suggest the steps that must be taken if the desired standards are to be reached. Bangladesh television 'made provision for every party fielding a minimum of thirty candidates to make a party political broadcast', with smaller parties being allocated thirty minutes and larger ones forty.[88] The otherwise weak print media in Sierra Leone nevertheless offered fair advertising at standard rates.[89] In St. Kitts and Nevis, the Commonwealth Observer Group noted that more remained to be done, 'in establishing fair and equal access for all political parties to (the state-owned radio and television services), for example, by developing formats which can enhance informed public discussion of political issues and balanced coverage of electoral campaigns.'[90] In Tanzania, the National Election Commission established guidelines on the question, although it was reported that little effort was made to ensure equitable access in practice.[91] Observers of the Russian presidential election in 1996, on the other hand, agreed that the 'regulatory framework for media coverage was detailed and clearly aimed at fairness'.[92] Equal access also seemed to work equitably in practice in Ghana,[93] but in Haiti little was done by the authorities to facilitate candidates' access to their two free hours of air time.[94]

---

[87] The author is grateful to Didier Maus for bringing these points to his attention.

[88] *The Parliamentary Elections in Bangladesh,* above note 75, 12-16. On allocation of time for party political broadcasts in the United Kingdom, see *Agenda for Change,* The Report of the Hansard Society Commission on Election Campaigns. Hansard Society, London, 1991, 52-3, and for the views of Labour and the Liberal Democrats, ibid., 83 and 90, respectively.

[89] *The Presidential and Parliamentary Elections in Sierra Leone,* above note 76.

[90] Commonwealth Observer Group, Commonwealth Secretariat, London, 1996. *The General Election in St. Kitts and Nevis,* 3 July 1995, 13.

[91] *The Union Presidential and Parliamentary Elections in Tanzania,* above note 78, 15. Amendments to the Elections Act in 1995 gave presidential candidates and political parties participating in elections the 'right to use' the state radio and broadcasting service during the official campaign period, and directed the NEC to co-ordinate the use of these rights.

[92] OSCE, 'Report on the Election of the President of the Russian Federation, 16 June and 3 July 1996', citing European Institute for the Media, 'Preliminary conclusions—Media coverage of the Russian presidential elections', 17 Jun. 1996. According to law, each candidate was entitled to 30 minutes free air time on each of the state-controlled television channels, allocated by the Central Electoral Commission by a random drawing: ibid., 10. See also report of the Norwegian Helsinki Committee to similar effect.

[93] National Democratic Institute, 'Ghana: Pre-Election Assessment', Accra, 19 Nov. 1996. Art. 55 of the Constitution provides that the State must allow a fair opportunity to all political parties to present their programmes to the public, by ensuring equal access to the state-owned media and that all presidential candidates should receive the same amount of time and space. The National Media Commission, which was constitutionally mandated to ensure press freedom and independence, promulgated guidelines on political reporting and equal access requirements. Ibid.

[94] Final Report of the OAS Electoral Observation Mission to the Legislative and Municipal Elections in Haiti (1995), s. 3.8.

The parties to the Dayton Peace Agreement undertook to 'ensure that conditions exist for the organization of free and fair elections, in particular... freedom of expression and of the press',[95] but in its August 1996 report the International Crisis Group remarked that 'the independent media continued to be hindered... (and) in the Republika Srpska there were no independent media at all'.[96]

2.2.3 Balance and bias in the media

As with the formal conditions of access, securing free speech and freedom of expression is also an area in which law and legal process can be especially effective, but may be inadequate to meet the challenges of harassment, intimidation and self-censorship. Harder still to regulate are the tone and quality of *coverage*, including the manner in which political events are reported, the analysis of political platforms and campaigns, and the criticism of parties and candidates. As Patrick Merloe has noted, 'Biased broadcast coverage... can shift the balance of political forces even where direct access broadcasting has been relatively fair.'[97]

A 1991 review of election campaigns in the United Kingdom noted that both main parties had advertisements rejected by newspapers in the opposite camp, on the grounds that they were misleading. In the view of the Hansard Society Commission, though this was a potentially worrying development,

> Partisanship in the press is nothing new... Bias in the tabloids is particularly marked: items favouring the preferred party find most space and unfavourable news may be omitted altogether. There is also an increasing tendency for the stories to consist mostly of 'smears' and 'knocking copy'. On the other hand, it is important not to overestimate the impact of the press...[98]

On the positive side, the Commonwealth Observer Group noted in one report that 'Bangladesh Television was scrupulous in giving equal exposure to the main parties during the campaign... (M)ost newspapers were not overtly partisan... A report on the activities of one political leader was balanced by a similar amount of space given to a rival... Both Bangla and English-language newspapers, with one or two exceptions, did not editorialise on who voters should support. Some... tended to show their support by the slant they gave to

---

[95] Annex 3, art. I(1).

[96] International Crisis Group, 'Elections in Bosnia and Herzegovina', Sarajevo, 13 Aug. 1996.

[97] Merloe, P., *Election Campaign Broadcasting in Transitional Democracies: Problems, Principles and Guidelines*, Article 19, 1994.

[98] *Agenda for Change*. The Report of the Hansard Society Commission on Election Campaigns. Hansard Society, London, 1991, 49-50.

their news stories and commentaries...'[99] In Sierra Leone, too, election coverage was more even-handed: 'Thirteen reporters were assigned to cover the campaign, with one assigned to each party on a rotation basis to avoid accusations of bias.'[100] In the United Kingdom, broadcasters have developed 'self-regulated conventions in their news and current affairs coverage based around "Stopwatch Timing";'[101] coverage is determined proportionately, according to the amount of air-time agreed for each party. Though this may provide a functional indicator of impartiality, and is generally defended by broadcasters, it tends to 'measur[e] words by their length rather than their weight or content'.[102]

Coverage by the publicly-owned services was noted as 'generally even-handed' in St. Kitts and Nevis, although ruling party activities tended to be reported first; both principal newspapers were party organs, however, 'clearly partisan, full of comment and opinion, sometimes vituperative, rather than factual independent reporting.'[103] Here, the question of focus had been taken up by church groups and was also dealt with in a Code of Conduct which stressed that public and private media should report the campaign honestly and impartially; ensure that news stories were accurate; and avoid the temptation to sensationalize reporting.[104]

Complaints about unfair and unbalanced coverage dominated the Russian presidential election in 1996, and were confirmed by independent observers.[105] In Zimbabwe, an independent weekly was reportedly pressured into firing an editor who had criticised the government,[106] while in Republika Srpska the ruling party's grip on the media was maintained, 'with regular purges to ensure unswerving loyalty among journalists'. When opposition parties were eventually allowed ninety minutes air time, under OSCE pressure, they were denied the opportunity to present their own programmes and subjected to tendentious questioning designed to promote the ruling party.[107]

---

[99]   *The Parliamentary Elections in Bangladesh,* above note 75, 16.

[100]   *The Presidential and Parliamentary Elections in Sierra Leone,* above note 76, 17. In the run-off second round to the presidential election, however, increasing government influence over the content of state radio news bulletins was noted: ibid., 32.

[101]   *Agenda for Change,* above note 98, 53.

[102]   Ibid.

[103]   *The General Election in St. Kitts and Nevis,* above note 90, 14.

[104]   Ibid., 13. For text of the Code of Conduct, see below, Annexe 7. On guidelines for election coverage by government-owned and private media in Tanzania, see *The Union Presidential and Parliamentary Elections in Tanzania,* above note 78, Annexes VIII and IX; reprinted below, Annexe 8.

[105]   OSCE, 'Report on the Election of the President of the Russian Federation, 16 June and 3 July 1996'; European Parliament Observers (Provisional Statement, 17 June 1996). In the direct language of the OSCE report, 'The undue influence which the Russian President exercised over the broadcast media may have constituted an abuse of his office, and the (OSCE) delegation recommends that further institutional controls be put in place to insulate the media and better equip it to conform with accepted standards of providing fair and balanced campaign coverage': ibid., 10.

[106]   Rotberg, Robert I, 'Democracy in Africa: The Ballot doesn't Tell All', *Christian Science Monitor,* 1 May 1996.

[107]   International Crisis Group, 'Electioneering in Republika Srpska', Aug. 1996.

In Bosnia and Herzegovina, the Provisional Election Commission promulgated regulations on the obligations of governments in relation to the media, standards of conduct for the media and journalists, and a Media Experts Commission to monitor compliance.[108] The International Crisis Group (ICG) reported that both RTV Bosnia and Herzegovina and RTV Srpska adopted the code of conduct, but that HTV Mostar did not. ICG referred to the Media Monitoring Report of the Institute of War & Peace Reporting:

> The essence of both sets of rules [adopted by RTV Bosnia and Herzegovina and RTV Srpska] is to specify equal principles and equal access in the coverage of parties' and independent candidates' election activities... Both broadcasters also pledge not to affirm or support those political parties and candidates who denigrate their opponents in the election campaign, let alone use any form of violence or intimidation against other parties during their participation in programmes... Differences appear in the policies which will determine the conduct of the broadcasters. RTV B&H's programme policy is to take into account the 'fact that B&H is a democratic, sovereign and politically and territorially independent state in which Bosniacs, Croats and Serbs are all constituent nations (together with others) and citizens.' SRT's policy, on the other hand, is to 'affirm the sovereignty and integrity of Republika Srpska, determined by the DPA'. SRT also declares that it 'will not present those political parties and factions whose programmes promote violent change of the constitutionally determined order of RS and threaten either its territorial integrity or the degree of independence which it has attained'.[109]

An OSCE Parliamentary Assembly statement that the state-owned media in Albania 'was not entirely unbiased' seemed somewhat disingenuous in the face of contemporaneous reports of the harassment of independent and opposition newspapers and journalists.[110] Even though the fact of incumbency is recognized as entailing significant electoral advantages, the National Democratic Institute in Ghana in 1996 found that the disparity in news

---

[108] Provisional Election Commission, Rules and Regulations, arts. 125—7, 128-36, 145-8. See further below, Annexe 5. A Media Experts Commission was also established under UNTAES, Part III, s. 2, with responsibility to assess 'the media coverage of the elections and the impact of such coverage on free and fair elections': UNTAES, Part III, s. 2. See also Part III, s. 1(2), under which the Transitional Administrator was authorised to take media coverage into account when certifying the elections: below, Annexe 1.)

[109] IWPR Monitoring Report, 10 Jul. 1996, 6, cited in International Crisis Group, 'Elections in Bosnia and Herzegovina', ICG Report, 22 Sept. 1996, 12-24. The ICG also noted that the 'most free' of the state-run media in Bosnia and Herzegovina was that in Bosniac-controlled territory; see also IWPR Monitoring Report, 4.

[110] OSCE Parliamentary Assembly report on the parliamentary elections in Albania, 26 May 1996, 1; on the human rights violations, see Human Rights Watch/Helsinki, Statement of Concern: Violations in the Albanian Elections, 30 May 1996, 3. Also, ODIHR, *Final Report*, Romanian Parliamentary and Presidential Elections, 3rd and 17th November 1996, s. 3.7.2, 'The Media: Television Coverage'.

- 27 -

coverage and tone in favour of the incumbent far exceeded what might have expected on that account.[111] Disparity of coverage was noted also in the 1996 Armenian presidential election, where the European Institute for the Media recorded some 1,050 minutes of editorial coverage of the incumbent candidate on state television's Channel 1, against 65, 48 and 37.5 minutes respectively for the next three candidates.[112]

2.2.4 Media responsibility and Codes of Conduct

A number of attempts have been made to encourage impartial and responsible reporting among the various media. For example, together with the Interim National Election Commission, the Sierra Leone Broadcasting Services developed a code of conduct in which it agreed that it should not become involved in personal attacks and character assassination.[113] The St. Kitts and Nevis code of conduct mentioned above emphasised honest, impartial and accurate reporting, and the avoidance of sensationalism. The Tanzanian National Electoral Commission issued guidelines for both state- and private-owned media (though it was unable to persuade opposition parties to sign on to a code of conduct for campaigning[114]); like the St. Kitts and Nevis model, the guidelines stressed that the state-owned media should report factual matters accurately and without bias, distinguish clearly between news and comment, and report controversial issues fairly. They 'urged' the private media to engage in fair reporting, and to provide a hearing for all sides on controversial issues.[115]

---

[111]   NDI, 'Ghana: Pre-Election Assessment', Accra, 19 Nov. 1996. The NDI was later to record its concern that 'the absence of mechanisms to ensure a more level playing field leaves room for future complaints': NDI, 'Preliminary Statement by the NDI International Observer Delegation to the December 7 Elections in Ghana', Accra, 10 Dec. 1996.

[112]   OSCE, Office for Democratic Institutions and Human Rights, 'Final Report. Armenian Presidential Election, September 22, 1996'; see also the Norwegian Helsinki Committee's report on the Russian presidential election, section 5.2: 'The state television broadcasts overwhelmingly favoured the incumbent president... Not only did (he) receive a very large part of the media coverage, but the information... was generally more positive than the coverage of the other candidates. In particular... (the) main challenger for the presidency... was very unfavourably treated in the state media.' See also Bulgarian Association for Fair Elections and Civil Rights, 'Mirror', (The Race for the Presidential Post mirrored in the Media, 2 issues, Oct., Nov. 1996), which examined the extent to which the media assured fair and equal access. Art. 47(10), Georgia Parliamentary Eleciton Law, aims to minimize the advantage of incumbents in terms of media coverage by restricting any addresses by the President, MPs and other officials related to the elections only to those broadcast times set aside specifically for the purpose: unofficial translation in Lansell, S.R. & Edgeworth, L.V., 'Republic of Georgia: Assessment and Voter Education Campaign, September-November 1995', IFES, Nov. 1996, Appx. D.

[113]   *The Presidential and Parliamentary Elections in Sierra Leone*, above note 76, 32.

[114]   *The Union Presidential and Parliamentary Elections in Tanzania*, above note 78, 14.

[115]   Much the same standards have been urged in other contexts; cf. Valentino, Henry, 'Establishing and Maintaining Balanced Media Support for Free and Fair Elections', *Elections Today*, vol. 5, no. 1, Dec. 1994, 10, and 'Guidelines for Media, Political Parties and Contesting Groups during Official Campaign Period for Municipal and Local Government Elections', drafted for use in Guyana, ibid., 12-13. The proposed guidelines cover, among others, news reporting, which should be factual, fair and without bias; professional care should be employed in the use and selection of news sources; and news analysis, commentary and editorials should be clearly identified as such (including the publication of disclaimers where appropriate). In the case of controversial public issues, fair representation should be given to opposing sides; equal access and equitable treatment should be accorded with regard to paid political messages; political parties and candidates must accept full responsibility for the content of materials produced or used; errors should be corrected; and where political advertisements are rejected, reasons should be given and an opportunity allowed to modify the material.

The impact of the guidelines was reportedly mixed, with some parties claiming they had not been informed and the ruling party claiming that the privately-owned media were against them.[116]

Observers to the Russian and Ghanaian presidential elections recommended further institutional controls, while the extent of bias led the International Crisis Group in August 1996 to come out against holding elections in Bosnia and Herzegovina.[117] In the last-mentioned case, notwithstanding the rules and regulations, the Media Experts Commission itself lacked power while the Provisional Election Commission showed little inclination to take the necessary action.

The 'standards of professional conduct' adopted with regard to Bosnia and Herzegovina are nevertheless instructive, particularly given the nature of the situation and the conditions in which elections were ultimately held.[118] Members of the media, 'as the servants of public interest', were called on to maintain the highest professional and ethical standards; to defend freedom of information and to distinguish clearly between factual reporting and editorial comment; to ensure that reports were factually accurate, complete, fair, equitable and unbiased; to avoid distortion, suppression, falsification, misrepresentation and censorship; to decline bribes or other inducement that might influence the exercise of their professional responsibilities; to avoid language that encouraged discrimination, ridicule, prejudice or hatred; to correct errors and inaccuracies promptly and to apologize and permit the right of reply where appropriate.[119]

The Canadian Daily Newspaper Association has adopted a statement of principles, expressing commitment to operate in the public interest and responsibility to the community. It recognizes freedom of the press as an exercise of the constitutionally protected individual right to freedom of expression, and that this right embodies 'the right to gather and disseminate information, to discuss, to advocate, to dissent'. A free press, in turn, 'enables readers to use their... right to receive information and make informed judgments on the issues and ideas of the time'.

On the operational side, newspapers should declare conflicts of interest, real or apparent, and guard their 'independence from government, commercial

---

[116]   Ibid., 18.

[117]   International Crisis Group, 'Elections in Bosnia and Herzegovina', 13 Aug. 1996, section III D (freedom of expression for the ruling parties only); E (political environment anything but neutral).

[118]   OSCE, Mission to Bosnia and Herzegovina, Provisional Election Commission, Rules and Regulations. Decisions until July 16, 1996.

[119]   Ibid., arts. 128-36. The Provisional Election Commission noted that the Standards derived from international agreements referred to in the Framework Section of the Dayton Peace Agreement, and the 1990 OSCE Copenhagen Document on the Human Dimension.

and other interests seeking to subvert content for their own purposes'. The statement continues:

> The newspaper keeps faith with readers by presenting information that is accurate, fair, comprehensive, interesting and timely. It should acknowledge its mistakes promptly and conspicuously. Sound practice clearly distinguishes among news reports, expressions of opinion, and materials produced for and by advertisers. When images have been altered or simulated, readers should be told...
>
> (T)he operation of a newspaper is a public trust and its overriding responsibility is to the society it serves. The newspaper plays many roles: a watchdog against evil and wrongdoing, an advocate for good works and noble deeds, and an opinion leader for its community. The newspaper should strive to paint a representative picture of its diverse communities, to encourage the expression of disparate views and to be accessible and accountable to the readers it serves, whether rich or poor, weak or powerful, minority or majority. When published material attacks an individual or group, those affected should be given an opportunity to reply...
>
> The newspaper should strive to treat the people it covers with courtesy and fairness. It should respect the rights of others, particularly every person's right to a fair trial. The inevitable conflict between privacy and the public good should be judged in the light of common sense and with decency.[120]

2.2.5 Compliance

This review of issues relating to the role and responsibilities of the media in time of elections has amply confirmed the necessity for standards of access and standards of conduct; it has also shown that, whereas rules can provide effectively for access, other or additional means may be called for in regard to coverage. The media can and should play an important part in realizing the existence of *choice*, and of allowing the electorate to act on an informed choice. At the same time, parties and candidates clearly know the power of the media in helping them to achieve the personal or political goal of securing public authority; human nature being what it is, one should not be too surprised to find that many of them seek to secure and exploit every possible advantage.

The performance of the media in recent years also shows the necessary tension that exists between the objective — advising the electorate about registration, voting, ballot procedures, and putting the electorate in the best position to make an informed choice, on the one hand — and the principles of

---

[120] Adopted by the Canadian Daily Newspaper Association in 1977, revised 1995.

free speech and a free and responsible media, on the other hand. Rules can provide the important framework, but tone and content, being matters of appreciation and personal preference, are more appropriate for regulation or influence on the basis of less directive models.

At both levels, the problem remains that of compliance. Rules relating to access and freedom of expression must be enforced, and a way must be found, if not to make a code *enforceable,* then to sanction its disregard in the most suitable way. Who proposes or develops such a code will clearly influence its overall acceptability. A code put forward by an electoral commission will be more likely to be accepted where there is already some confidence in the process.[121] A code that springs from the parties themselves, or from concerned citizens groups, might be more acceptable, particularly if it also clearly reflected a certain level of public expectation.[122]

The Media Experts Commission in Bosnia and Herzegovina, though it disappointed observers, was entrusted with responsibility, among others, to *monitor equitable access,* to *arrange for media monitoring* and to *consider complaints* of erroneous news reporting or the use of inflammatory language, and to *issue judgments* on such complaints, either insisting on their full publication by the media concerned or referring them to the Provisional Election Commission.[123]

An overly formal or heavy-handed mechanism may be self-defeating, however, and may explain the relative lack of success of the code in Bosnia and Herzegovina.[124] But unless the threat of some serious electoral disadvantage is present, the temptation to maximize control over the media and the content of publication will often become too great to resist. The

---

[121] Although opposition parties in Tanzania declined to subscribe to a campaign code of conduct proposed by the National Electoral Commission, fearing that it was a ruling party ploy to limit their activities, the Commission's guidelines for state- and privately-owned media appeared to have some positive impact; see *The Union Presidential and Parliamentary Elections in Tanzania,* above note 78, 14, 18.

[122] Cf. the experience in St Kitts and Nevis, where an alliance of church groups brokered a Code of Conduct for the Political Process, signed by four of the five political parties, followed by the establishment of a 'Committee to Promote Compliance: *The General Election in St. Kitts and Nevis,* above note 90, 12; the Commonwealth Observer Group considered that the Code had made 'a positive contribution in the highly polarised political climate': ibid. A group known as the People's Action Front for Free and Fair Elections (PAFFREL) was reported in Feb. 1997 to have urged the two main political parties in Sri Lanka to agree on a common code of conduct for elections, to ensure that party discipline is effectively enforced in the face of violent trends: *Sunday Times,* Sri Lanka, 16 Feb. 1997. Similarly, the Alliance of Seven Political Parties (ASPP) in Liberia in Jan. 1997 called on 'all political parties, political and other social leaders, armed faction leaders and former leaders, religious leaders, and interest groups and community leaders to commit themselves to' a national covenant under which they would agree to accept the outcome of the democratic electoral process, and for 'a level playing field', by which it meant fair and equal access to voters; freedom to speak and publicize views to voters without hinderance, and freedom to organize public meetings, etc., wherever elections are to be held: Statement of The Alliance of Seven Political Parties, Centennial Pavilion, Monrovia, 3 Jan. 1997: Document provided by ReliefWeb<http://www.reliefweb.int/>Date: 03 Jan 1997.

[123] Ibid., arts. 145-50.

[124] Cf. OSCE, Press Release, 'Election Appeals Sub-Commission Announces Decisions', 24 Aug. 1996; Press Release, 'Election Appeals Sub-Commission: Decisions taken in two cases of violations of voters' rights', 15 Aug. 1996.

challenge here again is to find public and effective sanctions; so far as compliance is and remains a matter for public sanction and to the extent that failure to abide by prescribed standards is likely to result in electoral prejudice, a code of conduct gives substance and meaning to the standards themselves, and provides a measure of accountability, reinforcing the responsibility of political parties, candidates and media workers themselves for actions, statements and consequences. The strength and effectiveness of a code of conduct, for the media as for political parties and candidates generally, thus resides in the extent to which it reflects, informs and appeals to a powerful body of public opinion.

2.2.6 Preliminary conclusions

The media have a special responsibility to report honestly and impartially on the election campaign, to ensure accurate reporting, and to distinguish editorial and commentary clearly. State-owned media, in particular, should also be impartial, while all media ought to allow equal access to eligible political parties. Members of the media, in turn, ought to conduct themselves professionally, defending freedom of information and resisting distortion, misrepresentation and censorship.

2.3 Election observation

'... States should take the necessary policy and institutional steps to ensure the progressive achievement and consolidation of democratic goals... In so doing, they should, among other matters... Ensure the registration of voters, updating of electoral rolls and balloting procedures, with the assistance of national and international observers as appropriate...' *Declaration on Criteria for Free and Fair Elections,* 4(2)

'... State authorities should ensure that the ballot is conducted so as to avoid fraud or other illegality, that the security and the integrity of the process is maintained, and that ballot counting is undertaken by trained personnel, subject to monitoring and/or impartial verification.' *Declaration on Criteria for Free and Fair Elections,* 4(6)

'States should take all necessary and appropriate measures to ensure the transparency of the entire electoral process including, for example, through the presence of party agents and duly accredited observers.' *Declaration on Criteria for Free and Fair Elections,* 4(7)

2.3.1 Election observation and international law

It is common knowledge that, so far as the organization of elections falls within the reserved domain of domestic jurisdiction, international law imposes no obligation on States to institute a national system of electoral observation, let alone to allow the entry and activities of international observers. The exceptional nature of United Nations electoral assistance has been reiterated in numerous General Assembly resolutions,[125] and yet the practical importance of election observation has also been recognized time and again.[126] Although no international instruments either require the observation of elections or regulate the rights, responsibilities and conduct of election observers,[127] 'best practice' increasingly recognizes the value of the exercise as a means of facilitating the internationally required result of a free and fair election, worthy of international support.[128] Indeed, the election-related commitments undertaken by OSCE States in Copenhagen in 1990 have been so interpreted as to give rise almost to an expectation of international observation. The OSCE Office for Democratic Institutions and Human Rights (ODIHR)[129] is to 'foster the implementation of paragraphs 6, 7 and 8 of the Document of the Copenhagen Meeting'. In addition to recognizing traditional political rights and the principle of free and fair elections on the basis of universal suffrage and secret ballot, participating States undertake, among others, to respect the right to establish political parties, to ensure that political campaigning can take place in a fair and free atmosphere, and that no obstacles stand in the way of

---

[125] See, for example, UNGA res. 50/172 (22 Dec. 1995), 'Respect for the principles of national sovereignty and non-interference in the internal affairs of States in their electoral processes', recognizing that the principles of national sovereignty and non-interference in the internal affairs of any State should be respected in the holding of elections, that the mechanisms and means to guarantee full and effective popular participation in electoral processes are for States to implement, and that UN electoral assistance should be provided only at the request and with the consent of States, under the authority of the Security Council or the General Assembly, or in special circumstances such as decolonization, or in the context of regional or international peace processes.

[126] See, for example, UNGA res. 50/185 (22 Dec. 1995), 'Strengthening the role of the United Nations in enhancing the effectiveness of the principle of periodic and genuine elections and the promotion of democratization', welcoming State support for UN electoral assistance activities by way of providing observers and contributing to the UN Trust Fund for Electoral Observation; UNGA res. 50/158 (21 Dec. 1995), 'Cooperation between the United Nations and the Organization of African Unity', urging continued UN support for the process of peaceful democratic transition, in particular, in regard to election observation. Notwithstanding the general principle that election processes are a matter of domestic jurisdiction, the General Assembly has also not hesitated to express its interest. See, for example, UNGA res. 50/178 (22 Dec. 1995), 'Situation of human rights in Cambodia', para. 6, urging the Government of Cambodia 'to promote and uphold the effective functioning of multi-party democracy, including the right to form political parties, stand for election, take part freely in a representative government and to freedom of expression'; UNGA res. 50/86 (15 Dec. 1995), 'The situation of democracy and human rights in Haiti', welcoming elections 'being held in a peaceful environment and observed by the Organization of American States in close coordination with the United Nations', and commending UN-OAS cooperation on, among other matters, election monitoring; UNGA res. 50/87 (18 Dec. 1995), 'Cooperation between the United Nations and the Organization for Security and Cooperation in Europe', welcoming joint UN-OSCE efforts in various areas, including election monitoring, and the important role assigned to the OSCE in supervising 'the preparation and conduct of free and fair elections in Bosnia and Herzegovina'.

[127] Cf. Cornillon, P., Secretary General of the Inter-Parliamentary Union, 'Rights and Responsibilities of Election Observers', paper presented to the International Conference in La Laguna on Freedom of Elections and the International Observation of Elections (Tenerife, 27 Feb.- 2 March 1994).

[128] Beibeder, Yves, *International Monitoring of Plebiscites, Referenda and National Elections*. Dordrecht, Martinus Nijhoff, 1994, 78, notes that the general elections in Moldvia and Walachia in 1857 were conducted under the supervision of a European Commission composed of Austrian, British, French, Prussian, Russian and Turkish representatives, which is possibly one of the first recorded instances of international election observation.

[129] The successor to the Office for Free Elections set up at the Paris Summit in 1990.

unimpeded access to the media. Moreover, recognizing that the presence of both foreign and domestic observers can enhance the electoral process, States, 'therefore invite observers from any other [OSCE] participating States and any appropriate private institutions and organizations who may wish to do so to observe the course of the national election proceedings, to the extent permitted by law'.[130] The mandate of the ODIHR was further strengthened at the 1994 Budapest Summit, when it was called on to undertake long-term observation. States are expected to notify ODIHR at least three months in advance, in order that the entire election cycle can be observed,[131] while other States are expected to provide the necessary long- and short-term observers.[132]

2.3.2 National observers

Although many States, for example, within the OSCE and the OAS, have been willing to accept international observers, the desirability of enhancing the role of national or domestic observers is no less important. As one commentator has remarked, 'Where any interested citizen may watch the count... democracy is most secure'.[133] National observers are perhaps the surest way by which to promote confidence in the electoral system overall, and the *right* to observe all aspects of a national election can be considered an essential component part of the general right to participate in public life. In practice, a system of national observers will have much in common with that which governs the deployment of international observers: accreditation and documentation; freedom of movement and freedom of access to all stages of the electoral process, including voter registration, the operation of polling stations during polling, the count and totalling and scrutiny (including the determination of claims made by candidates or their representatives) at each level. Equally, however, observers should not interfere with any stage of the ballot.[134]

---

[130] Document of the Copenhagen Meeting 1990, para. (8). Many States increasingly recognize the value of opening their electoral processes to observation at every level. As part of its international services strategy, Elections Canada is seeking amendments to the *Canada Elections Act* to allow international observation of Canadian elections: Elections Canada, *Serving Democracy,* Ottawa, 1994, 13.

[131] *The OSCE/ODIHR Election Observation Handbook,* 2nd ed., 1997; see also ODIHR, 'What Observers need to know about Election Administration', 'The Pre-Election Phase', and 'Election Phase: The Long- and Short-Term Observer', papers presented to the OSCE/ODIHR Seminar on Election Administration and Election Observation, Warsaw, 8-10 Apr. 1997.

[132] In practice, ODIHR often has difficulty in obtaining the necessary observers from other participating States; for example, though it requested eight long-term observers for the 1996 Presidential election in Bulgaria, only one was received: ODIHR, Bulgarian Presidential Election, October 27 and November 3, 1996 Final Report.

[133] Jones, George F., Director, Programs for the Americas, IFES, 'Fraud and Corruption in Elections and Election Campaigns', Address to the Seminar on Public Ethics sponsored by the Ministry of the Interior, Republic of Argentina, Buenos Aires, 10 Dec. 1996.

[134] See, for example, art. 3, Law on the Election of the President of the Republic of Moldova.

2.3.3 Terms of reference

One distinction between election observers and election monitors that has important practical implications is that those who *observe* generally do so passively, by being present, recording facts, receiving impressions, and reporting; while those who *monitor* may go further, by providing advice, guidance or warnings to election administrators, parties, candidates and electors, and by adding an element of supervision to the activity of fact-gathering otherwise shared with election observers.[135]

An election monitoring role is often assumed by a national electoral commission, by other officials charged with the national administration of an election, and by increasingly effective domestic observers. Both observers and monitors will likely engage in assessment or evaluation, but their reporting lines will usually differ; observers will submit their views to their sponsor, and often also to the host government and the media; while the responsibility of monitors is to the administering authority, which in turn is usually national, but may occasionally have an international dimension. For example, in Cambodia in 1992 the United Nations was actively engaged in administering and monitoring the election, and responsible also for ensuring compliance with the Code of Conduct.

In the absence of generally applicable rules and to the extent that every observation exercise depends in part upon its particular political context, it may help, as Pierre Cornillon has suggested, to look first at the responsibilities of election observers and thereafter to consider the rights and facilities required if they are to fulfil their task, and at the corresponding obligations that may fall upon them.[136] He, too, makes an important first point, namely, that election observation has nothing to do with technical assistance, and is not to be confused with the supervision or verification of elections. Observers are there to form an opinion on the electoral process, to 'guarantee' and support that process, or alternatively, to denounce and condemn an election that falls short of international standards; in this way, observers may contribute to the promotion of democracy in conformity with human rights.

The National Democratic Institute's 1996 pre-election assessment mission to Ghana, for example, had the following tasks: (1) to assess the legal framework for the elections and the election campaign environment against international standards for fair electoral competition and Ghanaian law; (2) to review the state of preparedness of the electoral administration; (3) to gauge the degree to which prospective voters were notified of the electoral process and about the candidates, so that they might make an informed choice; and

---

[135] Cf. Gould, R., Jackson, C. & Wells, L., *Strengthening Democracy: A Parliamentary Perspective,* Dartmouth, Aldershot, 1995, Ch. 8, Election Observation (based on papers by Horacio Boneo and Patrick Merloe).

[136] Cornillon, above note 127. See also *Strengthening Democracy,* above note 135, 55-64.

(4) to gauge the degree to which voters felt free to exercise their choice and had confidence in the electoral process to determine accurately and respect the will of the electorate.[137] The NDI/Council of Freely Elected Heads of Government Delegation to the Dominican Republic in May 1996 described its principal purpose as being,

> to demonstrate the international community's interest and support for the strengthening of the democratic processes in the Dominican Republic and to provide the international community with an objective assessment of the... electoral process... (T)he NDI/Council recognizes that Dominican citizens will ultimately determine the legitimacy of the... election as well as whether the results express the will of the electorate... The observer delegation will conduct its activities in accordance with the laws of the Dominican Republic and international standards and practices concerning electoral processes and electoral rights.[138]

The mandate of the OAS Electoral Observer Mission to Haiti in 1995 went somewhat further: 'to observe the organization and administration of the electoral process, to receive complaints of any irregularities brought to its attention and forward them to the competent bodies, to investigate the action taken regarding complaints and report on its observations to the competent authorities'. After discussions with the President of Provisional Electoral Council, it was agreed to allow 'observers to play a preventive role without impinging on the authority of the electoral agents'. The Mission would support every effort 'to ensure the integrity, transparency and credibility of the electoral process', and engage in problem-solving if the government requested.[139]

The mandates of recent Commonwealth observer groups, on the other hand, have been generally more circumspect. The terms of reference with regard to Bangladesh are typical:

> The Group is established by the Commonwealth Secretary-General at the request of the Government of Bangladesh and supported by the political parties. It is to observe relevant aspects of the organization and conduct of

---

[137] Statement of the National Democratic Institute for International Affairs (NDI) Pre-Election Assessment Delegation, Accra, 19 Nov. 1996

[138] NDI/Council of Freely Elected Heads of Government Delegation to the Dominican Republic, May 1996, Press Release, Carter Center, Atlanta, 10 May 1996.

[139] Unit for the Promotion of Democracy, Organization of American States, 'Establishment of the Electoral Observer Mission of the Organization of American States', 1995. The Mission was also 'to help increase confidence in the process through regular contacts and dialogue with the different sectors of society, in particular the candidates and political parties', and was authorised to publicize its observations and recommendations.

the election in accordance with the law of Bangladesh. It is to consider the various factors impinging on the credibility of the electoral process as a whole and to determine in its own judgment whether the conditions exist for a free expression of will by the electors and if the result of the election reflects the wishes of the people.

The Group is to act impartially and independently. It has no executive role; its function is not to supervise but to observe the process as a whole and to form a judgment accordingly. It would also be free to propose to the authorities concerned such action on institutional, procedural and other matters as would assist the holding of the election.[140]

However, the terms of reference for the mission to Pakistan in 1997, accepted by all the parties, included additionally the right to make recommendations for 'the effective functioning of the elected government.'[141] OSCE/ODIHR has also emphasised that it 'does not play the role of a judge, ruling on when the OSCE should "approve" an election. Rather, the ODIHR is there to support countries in democratic institution-building in line with agreed upon OSCE commitments. Its election reports, when critical, are not meant to condemn, but offer a balanced assessment of the entire process and recommendations for reform.'[142]

International observers, notes Pierre Cornillon, have responsibilities towards the international community and to the people of the country in question; it follows that their action must therefore be stamped by the mark of diligence, independence and impartiality.[143] This responsibility operates even before the moment of agreement to observe, for an invitation alone, or simple agreement to the presence of foreign observers is by no means sufficient. Potential observers must be confident that local law at least establishes the minimum formal conditions for holding a free and fair election; for it is within the framework of this law, moderated by reference to international standards, that the observer must work.[144] Inherent also in the nature of independent,

---

[140] Commonwealth Observer Group, *The Parliamentary Elections in Bangladesh, 12 June 1996*, Commonwealth Secretariat, London, 1997, 1. To identical effect, see the reports on *The General Election in St. Kitts and Nevis, 3 July 1995*, (1996), 1; *The Presidential and Parliamentary Elections in Sierra Leone, 26-27 February 1996*, (1996), 1; *The Union Presidential and Parliamentary Elections in Tanzania, 29 October 1995*, (1996), 1.

[141] Commonwealth Observer Group, *The General Election in Pakistan, 3 February 1997*, London, 1997, 2.

[142] *The OSCE/ODIHR Election Observation Handbook,* 2nd ed., 1997, 33.

[143] Cornillon, above note 127; see also Roel von Meijenfeldt, 'Election Observation', Report of an ECDPM Workshop, Maastricht, The Netherlands, 14-16 June 1995, Arnold Bergstraesser Institut: the basic rules for observers are neutrality and non-intervention in the process.

[144] Cf. Norwegian Helsinki Committee, *Manual for Election Observation,* (Rev. March 1996), including express references to 'reasonably peaceful circumstances' among the preconditions for dispatching observer missions, as well as a requirement that government concerned should invite and accredit election observers in good time before the elections. See also, Appendix 1: A Guide for Election Observers, in *Strengthening Democracy,* above note 135, 70-103, emphasising among others the importance of using *all* available information sources of information.

international observation is control over membership and scope; thus, the OSCE declined to send an observer mission to monitor the October 1996 local elections in Albania, after the government approved only part of the team.[145] An attempt to restrict an observation mission to a particular region of the country would be equally unacceptable.

2.3.4 Responsibilities and methods

The terms of reference and the objectives of the observers will largely determine their methodology. Their presence may be expected to contribute to both internal and external legitimation of the electoral process, and to confidence-building among the electorate; or to serve as a deterrent to electoral fraud and violence,[146] and a resource for problem and dispute resolution, especially if present over time.[147] Observers are expected, often to an unrealistic extent, to provide a prompt report and assessment on the basis of a single question: Was the election free and fair? Although there are times when such a determination is relatively easy to make, experience shows that a 'single judgment' is not always appropriate. For example, where elections are held as part of an overall peace settlement, majority rule might not be the best outcome in developmental terms, and relative judgments may have their place, at least where they in turn can be followed up by a process of continuous assessment.

In practice, international observers appear increasingly sensitive to the need to encourage democratic processes. Recent Commonwealth Observer Group reports, for example, have avoided simple judgments, preferring to use more nuanced language. The report on the 1997 general election in Pakistan described it as 'credible and that the conditions existed for a free expression of will by the people..., that while there were shortcomings these were not such as to affect the integrity of the process as a whole or the validity of the outcome..., that there was no evidence of systematic or widespread abuse'.[148] Similarly,

---

[145] Reuters, 16 Oct. 1996.

[146] In its Report on the Russian Presidential Elections in 1996, the Norwegian Helsinki Committee noted, 'Concern of possible fraud indeed seemed to be the only issue uniting the ten contenders. A main task of the election observation was therefore to verify or falsify these allegations, and to assess whether the published result of the polls could be assumed to reflect the will of the electorate.' It also considered that, 'The presence of a large number of *local* observers served to eradicate rumours and allegations of fraud and falsifications that had circulated prior to the elections. The broad presence of observers served to legitimise the result of the elections.' (Emphasis supplied).

[147] This is especially the case for pre-election assessment and technical assistance missions; see, for example, IFES, 'Uganda: A Pre-Election Assessment Report', Jan. 1996; IFES, 'Albania: A Pre-Election Technical Assessment', Aug. 1996; IFES, 'Toward Credible and Legitimate Elections in Kenya: Recommendations for Action', Apr. 1996; IFES, 'Republic of Georgia: Assessment and Voter Education Campaign, September-November 1995', Nov. 1996; also 'Statement of the National Democratic Institute for International Affairs (NDI) Pre-Election Assessment Delegation', Accra, 19 Nov. 1996.

[148] Commonwealth Observer Group, *The General Election in Pakistan, 3 February 1997*, London, 1997, 35. See also, *The General Election in St Kitts and Nevis, 3 July 1995*, 19: 'The result of the election reflected the wishes of the people'; *The Parliamentary Elections in Bangladesh, 12 June 1996*, 26-7: 'The conditions existed for a free expression of will by the voters and the results reflected the wishes of the people'; and compare more qualified conclusions in *'The Union Presidential and Parliamentary Elections in Tanzania, 29 October 1995'*, 25-6; *The Presidential and Parliamentary Elections in Sierra Leone, 26-27 February 1995*, 28-9.

the National Democratic Institute's preliminary statement on the December 1996 elections in Ghana avoided entirely any reference to a free and fair standard of elections, preferring instead to emphasize that 'the manner in which the elections... were conducted represents a positive step forward in the strengthening of Ghana's democracy and its electoral process'. It also complimented officials, the National Election Commission and the Inter-Party Advisory Committee, and noted 'the high voter turnout and the commendable level of citizen participation'. At the same time, this endorsement was accompanied by the practical (and non-confrontational) identification of problem areas, such as inequalities in state-owned media coverage of campaign activities, inadequate distribution of ballots in some parts of the country, and a series of recommendations that could enhance confidence and participation in future elections.[149]

At a Roundtable on election observation held in Stockholm in 1995, the participants were unable to agree on any 'uniform criteria for weighing the impact of irregularities and assessing the legitimacy of an election.'[150] And observers certainly have sometimes wondered whether the task was not too great.[151] A sense of the enormity of the problem at times can be gathered from experience with elections in Bosnia and Herzegovina. Immediately after polling in September 1996, the Co-ordinator for International Monitoring, Ed van Thijn, stated that although the elections had gone well technically, 'the general climate in which [they] took place was in some cases below the minimum standards of the OSCE Copenhagen Document.' The elections nevertheless offered 'a first and cautious step for the democratic functioning of the governing structures of Bosnia and Herzegovina', even though it was difficult to assess the process according to the term 'free and fair' as usually understood.[152] The International Crisis Group, however, had fewer doubts: 'the validity of these elections is in serious doubt, the results cannot be certified, and the elections must be rerun at a later date.'[153]

---

[149] National Democratic Institute, Press Release, 'Preliminary Statement by the International Observer Delegation to the December 7 Elections in Ghana', Accra, 10 Dec. 1996. The Commonwealth Observer Group also concluded its report on the Pakistan election with a number of practical suggestions: above note 148, 35.

[150] International IDEA, 'Lessons learnt: International Election Observation', Report on a Roundtable, Stockholm, 10-12 Oct. 1995, 13. In fact, this lack of consensus probably tells much about the reality, which is that observers necessarily come from a variety of cultures, all of whose political experiences and expectations will differ. This variety is part of the strength of democracy, and the best that one can or should hope for, perhaps, is (1) agreement on certain general principles (necessarily generalised in consequence at a certain level of abstraction); and (2) a clear account by those observing of *their* own principles and preconceptions.

[151] Cf. Klein, Keith, 'Election Observation in Tanzania: An Observer Asks if the Task is Too Great', *Elections Today,* Vol. 5, No. 4, Jan. 1996, 11-12, noting also the International Federation on Election Systems (IFES) decision not to make a post election statement on the free and fair issue, but rather (and in addition to its pre-election assessment) to issue a comprehensive analysis of the structure and how it worked.

[152] 'The Elections in Bosnia and Herzegovina, 14 September 1996,' Preliminary Statement of the Co-ordinator for International Monitoring (CIM), 16 Sept. 1996.

[153] Elections in Bosnia & Herzegovina, ICG Report, Sarajevo, 22 Sept. 1996, 32.

At a practical level, observers clearly have a duty to inform themselves. Commonwealth reports, for example, describe in detail the briefings provided to delegates in advance of departure, and include a short history and description of the political background in the country concerned, an analysis of the legal and administrative framework and an account of election preparations.[154] In other words, 'the responsibilities of observers include willingness to make preparations in advance, to be available for a sufficient length of time and to travel inside the country..., the capacity to understand a different and often complex national situation and to communicate by speaking at least a widely used language, if not the national language'.[155] To be credible, an electoral observation must also cover the process as a whole, including voter registration, campaigning, balloting, counting, tabulation and results.[156]

How election observation should be undertaken, and what should be observed, recorded and reported on, have all been amply developed at the practical level, in the grassroots experience of both national and international observers, and in the compilation of handbooks, guidelines and checklists.[157] *What* to observe may vary, from concentration on technical issues, such as constituency delimitation, voter registration, the secrecy of the ballot,[158] verification, and counting; to an assessment of the facts and variables of the election, including a record of the 'climate', and instances of violence, intimidation, and conflict,[159] the holding of rallies and meetings, access to and

---

[154] See, for example, Commonwealth Observer Group, *The Union Presidential and Parliamentary Elections in Tanzania, 29 October 1995*, (1996), 2-13; on observer training and deployment, see also Unit for the Promotion of Democracy, Organization of American States, 'Establishment of the Electoral Observer Mission of the Organization of American States', (1995).

[155] Cornillon, above note 127.

[156] Note in particular the ODIHR's practice of needs assessment and long- and short term observation; above note 131. See also International IDEA, 'Lessons learnt: International Election Observation', Report on a Roundtable, Stockholm, 10-12 Oct. 1995, 7, stressing *full coverage*, that is, process, not just polling; *impartiality*, which necessitates a direct relationship between the facts observed and the conclusions reached; *transparency*, which requires observers to 'state the underlying values and purposes' of the mission; and *professionalism*, that is, knowledgeable competence and ability.

[157] Much recent work owes its origins to Larry Garber's *Guidelines for International Election Observing*, first published in 1983 by the International Human Rights Law Group; see also by the same author, 'The Role of International Observers', in Garber, L. & Bjornlund, E., eds., *The New Democratic Frontier. A Country by Country Report on Elections In Central and Eastern Europe*, National Democratic Institute for International Affairs, Washington, 1992. At the practical level, see *The OSCE/ODIHR Election Observation Handbook*, 2nd ed., 1997; Council of Europe, *Handbook for observers of elections*, 1996; Norwegian Helsinki Committee, *Manual for Election Observation*, (Rev. March 1996; Appendix 1: A Guide for Election Observers, in *Strengthening Democracy*, above note 135, 70.

[158] Many observer reports have called attention to instances where secrecy was not assured. For example, Norwegian Helsinki Committee, Report on the Russian Presidential Elections 1996; Unit for the Promotion of Democracy-Organization of American States, Final Report of the OAS Electoral Observation Mission to the Legislative and Municipal Elections in Haiti (1995); Commonwealth Observer Group, *The Union Presidential and Parliamentary Elections in Tanzania, 29 October 1995*, (1996), 22, 25.

[159] A number of observers of the January 1996 elections in Palestine called attention to the 'chilling effect' of various security and public order regulations: National Democratic Institute for International Affairs and The Carter Center, 'Statement of the Second NDI/Carter Center Pre-Election Delegation to the 1996 Palestinian Elections', 16 Dec. 1995; Palestinian Centre for Human Rights and Robert F. Kennedy Memorial Centre for Human Rights, 'Joint Statement regarding Human Rights and Palestinian Elections', 19 Jan. 1996.

coverage by the media, and the possibilities and scope of campaigning. Considered from one perspective, observation has a critical *operational* or *functional* dimension: Recording facts, such as the presence of officials, party representatives and observers; or the availability of electoral materials, such as ballots, seals and receipts; or compliance with regulations, such as empty ballot boxes, the recording of serial numbers, the timely opening of polling stations, and so forth. Electoral facts also include security, orderliness, the absence or occurrence of violence, intimidation, pressure or propaganda, the effective resolution of disputes and the solving of problems.[160] Fulfilling these functional responsibilities means, as Pierre Cornillon also points out, that observers have related rights, including freedom of movement, the possibility of receiving and communicating information, and access to relevant documents and premises.[161]

From another perspective, observation always involves the *appreciation* of events, and their assessment and evaluation against standards often assumed to be universal, but effectively coloured by the observer's background and values. In a real sense, the fact of observation necessarily has an influence or impact on what is observed, and thereby engages further special responsibilities.

Thus, for example, the observer's independence requires disclosure and, like the candidate for office, transparency of financing. Neutrality and impartiality require that he or she not participate (though the inherently passive aspect to witnessing does not exclude either the entitlement to question voters, candidates, officials and others, or the obligation to bring problems or irregularities to the notice of the authorities);[162] that care be taken to prevent even the *appearance* of partiality or involvement, particularly in dealings with the media; that all those involved in the electoral process be brought with the area of contact. The observer's responsibility to report ultimately requires an assessment of events by reference to known standards and objectives, and on the basis of verifiable content and balance.

2.3.5 The rights and conduct of international observers

Armenian legislation on the status of foreign observers emphasizes, among others, their entitlement to be present at meetings of the electoral

---

[160] According to one view, a legal, investigative approach is to be encouraged, which is turn summarized as looking, asking questions, writing observations down, reporting, and not intervening at any stage: Roel von Meijenfeldt, 'Election Observation', Report of an ECDPM Workshop, above note 143, 10-11.

[161] Cornillon, above note 127. The Protocol concerning Elections in Palestine made detailed arrangements for accreditation and identification, freedom of movement and reporting.

[162] It is nevertheless essential that observers are 'visible'; voters, parties and officials should know observers are present, what their mandate is, and how to get in touch with them: Norwegian Helsinki Committee, *Manual for Election Observation,* (Rev. March 1996).

commissions, at the meetings of parties, and at polling stations; but it also provides that they do not have the right to engage in activities not related to the election campaign, that they should never interfere with the voting, counting or other electoral processes, and that though they can express their opinion, they have no right to attempt to alter or overturn the decisions of election officials.[163] Albanian law identifies who may be recognized as observers, confirms their freedom of movement and entitlement to ask, gather information and give opinions publicly, 'being impartial'.[164]

The Protocol concerning the elections in Palestine provided explicitly that 'the election process will be open to international observation. Observation will be conducted according to accepted international standards.'[165] It further provided that while observers' activity was limited to 'observation, reporting and dialogue', delegations 'may wish at any point to make comments or representations' to the Central Electoral Commission, which would consider them and reply appropriately. The Protocol laid down common terms of reference (for both international and domestic observers), and made detailed provision for the privileges and immunities of international delegations, including 'immunity from prosecution in respect of words spoken or written and any act performed by them in the exercise of their duties'.[166] Article 103(1) of the Election Law duly provided that the electoral process should be public and open to international and domestic observation.[167] Paragraph 2, in turn, made provision for the accreditation of local and international observers by the Central Election Commission, although this was reportedly a slow process for local monitors, particularly in the pre-election period. In fact, a substantial number of monitors were duly accredited and contributed significantly to the successful outcome.

Article 20 of the Russian Federal Election Law[168] provides that observers, including international observers, and representatives of mass media may be present at polling stations throughout election day.[169] Observers are also

---

[163]   Armenia, Regulations on the Status of Foreign Observers; translation available at **www.arminco.com.** Art. 153, Rules and Regulations for International Election Observers, adopted by the Provisional Election Commission for use in Bosnia and Herzegovina, provided that, 'International Observers will observe the electoral process in accordance with the Rules and Regulations of the Provisional Election Commission and they will not interfere in any way in electoral proceedings'. For full text, see below, Annexe 5.

[164]   Arts. 89, 90, 1996 Law for Assembly Elections; unofficial translation in DeGregorio, Paul S. & Ross, Kimberly L., 'Albania: Pre-Election Technical Assessment', IFES, Aug. 1996, Annex A.

[165]   Oslo: Interim Agreement, Annex II, Protocol concerning Elections, art. V.

[166]   Protocol concerning Elections, Appendix 3.

[167]   The Palestinian National Authority adopted the Election Law on 7 Dec. 1995.

[168]   Federal Law on Election of President of the Russian Federation, Passed by the State Duma on 24 Mar. 1995; approved by the Federation Council on 4 May 1995; signed by the President on 21 June 1995. Translation by International Federation on Election Systems (IFES) Election Resource Center in Moscow and available at **www.ifes.org**

[169]   Art. 14 provides that each candidate, electoral association, and electoral bloc may appoint one observer, who is entitled to remain at the voting premises from the beginning of voting to the completion of processing of documents on election results and to receive certified copies thereof. See also Rule 3, OSCE, Bosnia and Herzegovina, Rules for Registered Independent Candidate Representatives and Registered Political Party Representatives, adopted by the Provisional Election Commission, 10 May 1996.

entitled to be present at the voting of those who cannot come to the polling station for health or other good reasons; to familiarize themselves with the list of voters; to offer suggestions and remarks to polling station election commissions. However, no interference with the actions of the polling station election commission is permitted. On voting day, the empty ballot boxes are to be opened and displayed to the polling station election commission and to observers, and during voting the ballot box must remain in sight of the members of the polling station election commission and the observers.[170] A role for observers is also anticipated at other stages of the process, including inspection of unused ballots, counting, signing of the protocols, and publication of the results.[171]

The *behaviour* of international observers, apart from compliance with national law, is governed by general principles of accountability: to their mandate; to be professional; to be honest and impartial.[172] Observation *not* being purely external and removed, so there must be contact and consultation with the principal actors in the election process, including appropriate contacts and co-operation with national and other international observers.[173]

In an attempt to enhance the quality and performance of international observers, a code of conduct has also been proposed in their regard. Best practice, including the guidelines proposed by the Norwegian Helsinki Committee,[174] suggests the following principles as a minimum standard:[175]

Election Observers should:
1. Act in a strictly neutral and unbiased manner in relation to national authorities, parties and candidates, the voters, press and media, and the election observer's organization.
2. Refrain from any act in any way prejudicial to the election system, or to the administration of the election.
3. Disclose any fact that may give rise to a conflict of interests, or the appearance of a conflict of interest, during the observation and assessment.
4. Decline gifts from parties or persons involved in the election.
5. Comply with national laws and regulations, and the electoral code.

---

[170] Art. 51.

[171] Arts. 52, 58.

[172] Art. 155 of the Rules and Regulations for Bosnia and Herzegovina (above, note 163), expressly provided that 'International Observers shall be strictly impartial and politically neutral'.

[173] Cf. International IDEA, 'Lessons learnt: International Election Observation', Report on a Roundtable, Stockholm, 10-12 Oct. 1995, 8, 16-20.

[174] Norwegian Helsinki Committee, *Manual for Election Observation,* (Rev. March 1996).

[175] See also the observer code of conduct proposed in *The OSCE/ODIHR Election Observation Handbook,* 5-6; reproduced below in Annexe 16.

6. Be cautious in sharing information gathered during the observation, and avoid premature conclusions.

7. Base all conclusions on verifiable, factual evidence, and use agreed standards of reference.

2.3.6 Preliminary conclusions

Election observation, both national and international, can help to ensure that polling proceeds fairly and without fraud. At the national level, the participation of domestic observers as a regular feature of all aspects of the electoral process also enhances public confidence in the system and is likely also to encourage inter-party co-operation and thereby reduce occasions of friction and possible violence. Effective election observation depends, among others, on a measure of institutionalization, including accreditation, as well as on appropriate guarantees of access, communication and freedom of expression. Observers themselves, however, also have responsibilities and, while they should be able to convey their concerns to the appropriate authorities, should not otherwise interfere in the election. International observers should maintain a position of neutrality, binding themselves also to appropriate principles of disclosure and transparency.

2.4 Elections and fair campaign practices

'Everyone individually and together with others has the right: To express political opinions without interference; to seek, receive and impart information and to make an informed choice; To move freely within the country in order to campaign for election; To campaign on an equal basis with other political parties, including the party forming the existing government.' *Declaration on Criteria for Free and Fair Elections,* 3(3)

'The right of candidates to security with respect to their lives and property shall be recognized and protected.' *Declaration on Criteria for Free and Fair Elections,* 3(5)

'Candidature, party and campaign rights carry responsibilities to the community. In particular, no candidate or political party shall engage in violence.'

'Every candidate and political party competing in an election shall respect the rights and freedoms of others.' *Declaration on Criteria for Free and Fair Elections,* 3(9),(10).

'States shall respect and ensure the human rights of all individuals within their territory and subject to their jurisdiction. In time of elections, the State and its organs should therefore ensure...That freedom of movement, assembly, association and expression are respected, particularly in the context of political rallies and meetings...'

'In order that elections shall be fair, States should take the necessary measures to ensure that parties and candidates enjoy reasonable opportunities to present their electoral platform...' *Declaration on Criteria for Free and Fair Elections,* 4(3),(4)

'States should take the necessary measures to ensure that parties, candidates and supporters enjoy equal security, and that State authorities take the necessary steps to prevent electoral violence.' *Declaration on Criteria for Free and Fair Elections,* 4(8)

The notion of 'fair campaign practices' is sufficiently broad to encompass the responsibilities of government authorities, electoral commissions, political parties, candidates, and their supporters. It covers how the electoral campaign is conducted, as well the facts that contribute to or undermine the confidence of voters and participants in the integrity of the process as a whole. While rules of law have a direct effect on the conduct of an election, for example, by prohibiting violence or the threat of violence, more general standards may be needed to ensure that the *tone* of the campaign remains at a level conducive to an effective exercise of the right to vote.

Some Codes of Conduct, for example, those with a United Nations or international background, underline the necessity for parties, members, candidates and sympathizers to 'promote conditions conducive to the conduct of free and fair elections, and a climate of democratic tolerance in which political activity may take place without fear of coercion, intimidation or reprisals'.[176] Others aim to influence content and conduct, emphasizing that criticism of other political parties should be confined to their policies, programmes and record; that leaders and candidates should not be criticised in regard to their private life unconnected with public activities, and that criticism should not be based on mere allegations.[177] The Code adopted for St Kitts and Nevis stressed 'issues rather than personalities', that candidates 'must seek to be truthful about the past and present socio-economic state', and 'avoid raising unfulfillable expectations and making unrealistic promises.'[178]

Notwithstanding the general applicability of the criminal law to violence at election time, each Code reiterates not only the unacceptability of such events, but also the responsibility of parties, candidates and workers to ensure that a peaceful climate is maintained. Thus, they are frequently called on

---

[176] See, for example, UNTAES, para. 1; Bosnia and Herzegovina, art. 119; also, Seychelles, s. 1(5); Bangladesh 1991, s. 5. The references to Codes of Conduct in this section are to those reproduced in the Annexes.

[177] India, s. I(2); Panama, s. 3; Pakistan, s. (14); St. Kitts and Nevis, s. B; Ghana, s. 8; Seychelles, s. 1(6), (7).

[178] St. Kitts and Nevis, s. B. The Commonwealth Observer Group, however, reported that 'Personalities rather than issues dominated the political campaign with personal invective a common feature... It says something for the overall peaceful nature of the electoral environment that despite this personal invective, there were relatively few incidents of unruly behaviour or violence.' *The General Election in St Kitts and Nevis, 3 July 1995,* 11-12.

publicly to condemn violence and intimidation,[179] to prevent or avoid language or conduct that may lead to violence or intimidation,[180] or that may exploit or aggravate existing differences at community level,[181] and not to disrupt each others' meetings and processions. Such directions are also frequently linked to the principle of 'reciprocal respect', expressly conditioning the exercise of political rights on respect for the right of other parties and candidates to conduct their own campaigns in a peaceful environment and to have access to potential voters.[182]

2.4.1 The responsibility of political parties and candidates

The responsibility of political parties and candidates in particular is emphasized in, among others, the Electoral Code promulgated by the United Nations Transitional Administration in Eastern Slavonia, Baranja and Western Sirmium. They are to 'discipline and restrain' their members and sympathizers from committing any violation of law or procedure and, in addition to publicly condemning violence and rejecting discrimination, they 'commit themselves' to promote free and fair elections, encourage the free expression of the will of the electorate, give wide publicity to the Code, promote accurate information on the electoral processes, and reassure sympathizers and voters about the impartiality of the electoral administration, the secrecy and integrity of the ballot.[183] In adjudicating complaints and providing opinions for action, the Election Appeals Commission is in turn entitled to take into account the responsibility of party leaders and candidates for the actions of their members and sympathizers.[184]

Given the emotions and the frequently divisive effect of electoral campaigns, this emphasis on non-violence and non-inflammatory language is

---

[180] UNTAES, Part 1, ss. 7, 8, 9; India, s. I(1); Panama, s. 3; Pakistan, para. 21; Bosnia and Herzegovina, art. 122; Cambodia, para. 4(6); Ghana, para. 11; Seychelles, s. 1(7); Bangadesh 1991, ss. 6, 7, 8.

[179] UNTAES, Part 1, s. 4; Liberia, para. 3(a); Cambodia, para. 4; Seychelles, s. 1(8); Bangladesh 1991, s. 8.

[181] UNTAES, Part 1, s. 4, requires participants to commit themselves to 'reject any form of discrimination based on race, gender, ethnicity, language, class or religion in connection with the elections and political activity'; India, s. I(1), that 'No party or candidate shall indulge in any activity which may aggravate existing differences or create mutual hatred or cause tension between different casts and communities, religious or linguistic'; India, s. I(3), that 'There shall be no appeal to caste or communal feelings for securing votes'; see also Bangladesh 1996, s. 17; Pakistan, s. 17; Ghana, para. 9. The Protocol concerning the Palestinian elections provided that 'Each side shall take all necessary measures with regard to persons under its authority to prevent public disorder during campaign activities..., and to protect the electoral process from any violence, incitement, hostile propaganda or other undemocratic interference': art. IV, 2(d)

[182] UNTAES, Part 1, s. 9; Liberia, para. 3. See also Pakistan, para. 19: 'Public leaders and other participants in political activity shall act with a sense of responsibility and dignity befitting their status. While propagating their own views and programmes, they shall not interfere with the freedom of others to do the same as that would be the negation of democracy'; also, Bosnia and Herzegovina, art. 122; Cambodia, para. 9; Ghana, paras. 3, 10; Seychelles, para. 3; Bangladesh 1991, para. 3.

[183] UNTAES, Part 1, ss. 2, 4, 12.

[184] UNTAES, Part 14, ss. 5, 6. On party and candidate responsibility, see also Bosnia and Herzegovina, art. 119.

hardly surprising, and recognition of the continuing need to improve the climate is clear from recent experience. The 1995 campaign in St. Kitts and Nevis followed violent clashes and a short state of emergency after the inconclusive results of the 1993 general election, and also the emergence of violent, especially drug-related crime, as a political issue. The Code of Conduct was promoted because, as its preamble noted, 'electioneering is potentially divisive, and in the heat of campaigning it may be forgotten that we are one people'. In the event, tolerance and good humour prevailed, notwithstanding the tendency to personal invective.[185] Again, in the view of the Commonwealth Observer Group, much of the credit went to the Committee to Promote Compliance with the Code of Conduct, which met daily to consider reports of violations and to recommend corrective action.[186]

The February 1996 elections in Sierra Leone likewise took place against a background of violence, including five years of civil war and two coups. They were held also after the failure of last-minute efforts to achieve peace first, and despite concerns that adequate security could not be provided. The Commonwealth Observer Group noted that co-operation between the parties 'did... much to make the campaign free of violence and intimidation',[187] and led also to agreement on a *de facto* code of conduct. On the other hand, the campaign in Sierra Leone was run mainly on the basis of personalities, with little if any debate of policy issues.[188] Negative campaigning characterised the press coverage of the second round of the Presidential election, although it too was completed generally without violence or intimidation.[189]

The Commonwealth Observer Group to the 1996 Parliamentary Elections in Bangladesh noted that they had been 'widely expected to be marred by violence, intimidation, vote-rigging and other improper practices'.[190] The installation of a caretaker government and the appointment of a new Chief Election Commissioner, however, provided an essential neutral moment,[191] and a Code of Conduct was drafted by the Election Commission after discussion with the political parties.[192] The campaign took place in a 'relatively peaceful and non-confrontational environment', although there were some reports of 'strong-arm tactics and intimidation, including

---

[185] Commonwealth Observer Group, *The General Election in St Kitts and Nevis, 3 July 1995*, (1996), 11-12.

[186] Its recommendations included a ban on motorcades following several violent incidents: ibid., 12.

[187] A number of attacks were launched by rebel forces, however, causing the abandonment of several planned polling stations: Commonwealth Observer Group, *The Presidential and Parliamentary Elections in Sierra Leone, 26-27 February 1996*, (1996), 33.

[188] Ibid., 19-20.

[189] Ibid., 31-2.

[190] Commonwealth Observer Group, *The Parliamentary Elections in Bangladesh, 12 June 1996*, (1996)3.

[191] Ibid., 5-6.

[192] Ibid., 11.

harassment of women and minority communities'.[193] Again, however, there was little discussion of policy issues.[194]

2.4.2 Restrictions on political activity and speech

The Commonwealth Observer Group to Pakistan in 1997 found a somewhat subdued campaign, attributable in part to seasonable factors, but also to 'considerable public cynicism regarding the honesty and effectiveness of the leaders of the major parties'.[195] Karachi, scene of past electoral violence, witnessed no serious disturbances, mainly as a result of the strategic deployment of security forces,[196] although the Observer Group received complaints from one party that it was unable to campaign freely because of the state's failure to protect it from attack. In the lead-in to the 1997 Algerian elections, on the other hand, political violence was identified by Human Rights Watch as a major factor in the way of free and fair elections.[197]

Ironically, successful efforts to promote a peaceful election may have a down side. The various restrictions collected and recalled in the Pakistan Code of Conduct were credited with having had a dampening effect on the campaign.[198] In Bangladesh, too, the Code of Conduct undoubtedly contributed to the generally calmer atmosphere; for example, posters were limited in size, hoardings banned, wall-writings prohibited, and further limits placed on acceptable activity (no over-pasting or use of motor vehicles, restrictions on microphone use).

Some types of restriction of political activity, particularly limitations on content or electoral propaganda generally, may thus have the effect of frustrating public debate, steering the election campaign away from potentially divisive policy issues; as in so many areas of competing rights and freedoms, the art is to find a balance between a peaceful campaign and the free (and often passionate) expression of opinion.

In one 'free' environment for expression, in particular, the question of fair campaign practices has also been much debated.[199] One commentator called attention to the 'disastrous effects on the quality of both speech and politics of

---

[193]   Ibid., 12, 14-15, 32-3.

[194]   'the campaign was... fought on accusations of misdeeds, corruption, incompetence and obstruction on the part of each of the main parties. They also charged each other with planning to rig the polls. No attempt was made to answer the accusations in any meaningful way': ibid., 15.

[195]   Commonwealth Observer Group, *The General Election in Pakistan, 3 February 1997,* (1997), 20.

[196]   Ibid., 22.

[197]   Human Rights Watch, 'Algeria-Elections in the Shadow of Violence and Repression,' 20 May 1997.

[198]   Ibid., 21.

[199]   See Carville, J. & Matalin, M., *All's Fair: Love, War and Running for President,* Random House, 1994. Touchstone, 1995; Sterline, B., 'Merchants of Venom', *Wired,* May 1996, 65.

unfettered political advertising on television... (I)mages have replaced issues, the periphery has replaced the pertinent; demagoguery has replaced dialogue; distortion has supplanted discussion'.[200] Others have found that political advertisements are more informative than manipulative, although their main effect may be to reinforce, not change, existing political predispositions.[201] 'Negative' or 'attack' advertising, on the other hand, seems to be growing in popularity, as was especially apparent in the U.S. in 1996, when such campaigning attracted considerable media comment, both in the Presidential election and in the primaries.[202] Such tactics, which have been variously attributed to candidates' fear, the competitive nature of campaigns, the activities of organized interests, and the style of media coverage, have also been credited with contributing to voter disenchantment.[203] Many have called for an end to such 'sleazy tactics'. For example, the Secretary of the Florida Department of State, Sandra B. Mortham, urged that candidates take responsibility for the work of their campaign staff and supporters; campaign materials should therefore all be approved by candidates, or carry a disclaimer stating that they were not approved. In addition, it was proposed that a Fair Campaign Practices Board be established, in order to reach better compliance with election laws and 'common decency' in campaigning. The Board would review complaints during the campaign, on the basis of a code of conduct voluntarily signed by all candidates. In the United States, however, constitutional constraints preclude legislation and penalties for failure to comply with such a code; the only sanction, therefore, would be through media reports of a candidate's breach or non-compliance with a ruling of the Board.

---

[200] Curtis Gans, Vice-President and Director, Committee for the Study of the American Electorate, Evidence to the US Senate Subcommittee on Communications on the *Clean Campaign Act*, May 1993. He noted also that political advertising has been 'the driving force in making campaigns so expensive and making politics accessible only to the wealthy or those with access to broad individual or interest group wealth.' Evidence also suggests that excessive money in politics leads to voter disenchantment; less than half of all eligible voters cast ballots in the 1996 US elections.

[201] Ansolabehere, Stephen & Iyengar, Shanto, *Going Negative: How Political Advertisements Shrink and Polarize the Electorate,* The Free Press, New York, NY, 1995; review by Maris LeBlanc McCrory, *The Guardian* (Journal of the Council on Governmental Ethics Laws—COGEL), December 1996, 1,3. During the 1996 Romanian elections, the ruling party produced a television clip accusing the opposition presidential candidate of calling for the return of the former sovereign; it showed the candidate's face turning into that of the king. The opposition responded with, though it quickly withdrew, a similar clip in which the incumbent president's face turned into that of former president Ceausescu: Office for Democratic Institutions and Human Rights, *Final Report,* Romanian Parliamentary and Presidential Elections, 3rd and 17th November 1996.

[202] See, among many examples, Balz, D. & Edsall, T.B., 'More Shouts and Smears as the Querulous Republicans Debate', *International Herald Tribune,* 2-3 Mar. 1996; Berke, R.L., 'Attack Ads Arouse Anger', ibid., 17-18 Feb. 1996; Bennet, J., 'Who's Negative? Check Clinton Ads', *International Herald Tribune,* 23 Oct. 1996; Kurtz, H., 'The Man behind the Voices that Keep Shrieking "Liberal",' ibid.

[203] See Ansolabehere & Iyengar, *Going Negative: How Political Advertisements Shink and Polarize the Electorate,* above note 201. A Republican candidate for nomination, Steve Forbes, was reported to have lost support for having broadcast so many advertisements critical of his opponents: *International Herald Tribune,* 16, 17-18 Feb. 1996.

The potential difficulties in regulating the content and tone of comment in an election are only too well evident in any State that adheres to constitutional principles of free speech. This is again well illustrated by the experience of the United States where, although the doctrine of fairness and equal opportunities has been integrated into the law and practice of broadcast media, the same does not apply to print. Under U.S. law, the Federal Communications Commission is responsible for ensuring, amongst others, that radio and television licensing serves the 'public interest', while the Commission's doctrine of fairness 'requires every broadcaster to afford a reasonable opportunity for the presentation of contrasting viewpoints on controversial issues of pubic importance'; this means that coverage must be adequate and fair, and accurately reflect opposing views.[204] Attempts to apply similar principles, even including a statutory 'right of reply', to the print media have been struck down as unconstitutional,[205] while the control of the content of broadcast political advertisements on the basis of an 'indecency standard' has also proven problematic.[206]

The quality of an election is frequently damaged by intimidation and corruption. In most countries, such matters are dealt with in legislation. The Pakistan Representation of the People Act prohibits, among others, bribery, intimidation, and impersonation.[207] In the United States, it is an offence under the Criminal Code to pay, or to solicit or receive money or other consideration in return for the promise to support a person for appointment to a federal office.[208] It is also an offence to place troops at any polling place or, as a member of the armed forces, to attempt to prescribe or fix the qualifications of voters at any election, or by force, threat, intimidation or otherwise to prevent or try to prevent any qualified voter from casting his or her ballot, or to compel the acceptance of any ballot;[209] and for anyone to intimidate voters, or 'to make an expenditure to any person, either to vote or withhold his vote, or to vote for or against any candidate'.[210]

---

[204] Durbin, Thomas M., 'Extending the Fairness Doctrine to the Print Media', CRS Report for Congress, 17 Jun. 1987, 1,3. The constitutionality of the fairness doctrine as it applies to broadcast media was upheld by the US Supreme Court in *Red Lion Broadcasting Co. v. Federal Communications Commission*, 395 U.S. 367 (1967).

[205] Ibid., 7-9. In *Miami Herald Publishing v. Tornillo*, 418 U.S. 241 (1974), the US Supreme Court concluded that the First Amendment prohibited any legislation requiring the press to publish what it would not otherwise print.

[206] See Paige Whitaker, L., 'Political Broadcasting Laws and the Indecency Standard: The Issue of Campaign Advertisements Featuring Dead Fetuses and Abortion Procedures', CRS Report for Congress, 14 Jul. 1993.

[207] See below, Annexe 3, Pakistan, Code of Conduct, para. 25.

[208] 18 U.S.C. §§210, 211; see also on promises or support for public or private employment, or to deprive of employment: §§599, 600, 601. A useful summary of the law is found in *Senate Election Law Guidebook 1996*, A Compilation of Senate Campaign Information, including Federal and State Laws governing Election to the United States Senate, U.S. Government Printing Office, Washington, 1996.

[209] 18 U.S.C. §593. Cf. OSCE, Office for Democratic Institutions and Human Rights, Final Report, Armenian Presidential Election, 22 Sept. 1996, noting that, 'In many cases observers witnessed officers either instructing or leading their troops to vote for Levon Ter-Petrossian.'

[210] Ibid., §§594, 597.

Of relevance to campaigning, the Criminal Code declares it an offence to use government funds for 'work relief, relief, or for increasing employment by providing loans and grants for public-works projects... for the purpose of interfering with, restraining, or coercing any individual' in the exercise of his or her right to vote.[211] Similar criminal sanctions attach to certain instances of solicitation of political contributions; to the use of military authority to influence the vote of members of the armed forces: and to the intimidation or coercion of federal employees.[212]

The 1996 Bangladesh Code of Conduct accepted that political parties may publish their overall development planning, but from the date of announcement of the election schedule until polling is completed, parties and candidates 'may not donate or commit to donate any sum of money, publicly or secretly, to any institution of their respective constituencies'.[213] Campaign expenditure was also limited to approximately $7,500 for each candidate in each constituency.[214] India's Code of Conduct addresses one chapter specifically to the 'party in power', providing that 'ministers and other authorities shall not sanction grants/ payment out of discretionary funds from the time elections are announced' by the Election Commission, announce any financial grants, lay any foundation stones, or make any promise of construction of roads, provision of drinking water, and so forth. That there might be a 'moral' or 'illegitimate' dimension to such activities was not apparently shared by some politicians in Singapore. In December 1996, for example, the Prime Minister was reported as stating that it was not unfair for the ruling party to use public funds to upgrade housing projects in wards which supported it. A later report noted that, with vote counting now decentralised within a ward, MPs could tell where the support was coming from and who would therefore get upgrading first.[215]

In Republika Srpska, the International Crisis Group noted that the ruling Srpska demokratska stranka (SDS) was involved in pressuring the electorate, particularly displaced persons, through the allocation of housing, jobs and humanitarian assistance. Opposition parties complained that they also were increasingly under pressure, including through attacks on individuals and facilities, to stop their activities.[216] In August 1996, the Election Appeals Sub-

---

[211] Ibid., §598.

[212] Ibid., §§ 602-607, 609, 610.

[213] Bangladesh Election Commission, Code of Conduct for Political Parties and Candidates (May 1996): text in Commonwealth Observer Group, *The Parliamentary Elections in Bangladesh, 12 June 1996*, (1997), 56; and below Annexe 4. The Code declares also that, 'Election shall not be influenced by money, weapons, muscle power or local influence.' Cf. Statement of the National Democratic Institute for International Affairs, Pre-Election Assessment Delegation, Ghana, Nov. 1996, referring to reports that State resources were being used to secure electoral advantages, including dedication ceremonies and government contracts.

[214] Commonwealth Observer Group, *The Parliamentary Elections in Bangladesh, 12 June 1996*, (1997), 14.

[215] *Straits Times*, 28 Dec. 1996, 1 Jan. 1997.

[216] International Crisis Group, 'Electioneering in Republika Srpska', ICG Bosnia Project, Sarajevo, Aug. 1996, 6; see also Press Release, 4 Dec. 1996, 'ICG Cautions Against Further Electoral Engineering in the Run-up to the Municipal Elections'.

Commission (EASC) investigated the case of linking humanitarian assistance to voter registration in the municipality of Dobroj and, even though international pressure appeared to have halted implementation of the policy, it found the SDS in violation of the Dayton Peace Agreement. The EASC imposed a penalty of 25 per cent of the party's entitlement to campaign funds and ordered it to give a public apology to the victims.[217] In other decisions, the EASC confirmed that political parties and candidates have the right to create and distribute posters and leaflets, and censured police in Bihac for having confiscated campaign materials; it condemned all politically motivated violence, and advised that wherever such violence or intimidation occurs, the ruling party or other party that most stands to benefit is obliged to publish statements condemning such acts and to instruct its members and supporters that it will not be tolerated; and it further condemned an increasing number of incidents of employment-related intimidation, dismissals and threatened dismissals against opposition party politicians and supporters.[218]

In other countries, legal provisions covering the same or similar ground are often recalled in less technical language in the Code of Conduct, as the examples in the Annexes show. So much can go wrong or be distorted in the electoral process, that it is too important to be left to 'form' alone. A successful election, translating the will of the people, requires 'a climate of *equitable* implementation', and that may best be developed through the complementary actions of law and codes of conduct, moderated by the influence of an independent and impartial authority. The value of a code, in particular, lies also in the extent to which it creates or endorses public expectations in relation to electoral behaviour, even if it is formally unenforceable.

2.4.3 Preliminary conclusions

A fair electoral campaign is contingent, in particular, on the absence of violence and intimidation, and government, parties and candidates are responsible for a peaceful environment in which views can be exchanged, voters canvassed and platforms disseminated. This includes avoiding abuse or inflammatory language and co-operating with the police or other authority in the organization of meetings and processions. Fair campaign practices in turn depend on the recognition of others' rights, including the freedom of all to campaign for election. In order to encourage democratic debate on political issues relevant to the election, participants should avoid personal and unverified criticism. Parties and candidates should also accept responsibility for the activities of their staff and sympathizers, committing themselves and

---

[217] OSCE, Mission to Bosnia and Herzegovina, Press Release, 15 Aug. 1996.

[218] OSCE, Mission to Bosnia and Herzegovina, Press Release, 24 Aug. 1996.

their staff and sympathizers to comply with election laws and to campaign standards of decency and fairness.

2.5 The institutionalization of electoral process

'Every candidate and political party competing in an election shall accept the outcome of a free and fair election.' *Declaration on Criteria for Free and Fair Elections,* 3(11)

'States should take the necessary legislative steps and other measures, in accordance with their constitutional processes, to guarantee the rights and institutional framework for periodic and genuine, free and fair elections, in accordance with their obligations under international law.' *Declaration on Criteria for Free and Fair Elections,* 4(1)

'In addition, States should take the necessary policy and institutional steps to ensure the progressive achievement and consolidation of democratic goals, including through the establishment of a neutral, impartial or balanced mechanism for the management of elections...' *Declaration on Criteria for Free and Fair Elections,* 4(2)

'States should take all necessary and appropriate measures to ensure the transparency of the entire electoral process including, for example, through the presence of party agents and duly accredited observers.' *Declaration on Criteria for Free and Fair Elections,* 4(7)

'States should ensure that violations of human rights and complaints relating to the electoral process are determined promptly within the timeframe of the electoral process and effectively by an independent and impartial authority, such as an electoral commission or the courts.' *Declaration on Criteria for Free and Fair Elections,* 4(9)

The basic human and political rights that constitute the foundation for democratic and representative government derive their force from both treaty and customary international law; to some extent, these indicate the content of the *general* obligations of States in the matter of implementation of the individual's right to participate in public life and related duties with regard to elections.[219] The question remains, however, what exactly States are required to do in their municipal law and administrative arrangements, particularly in the absence of any express reference to legislative incorporation or any other formal implementing step.

---

[219]   For an examination of the international law dimensions to elections, see Goodwin-Gill, G.S., *Free and Fair Elections: International Law and Practice,* Inter-Parliamentary Union, Geneva, 1994.

The *general* duty of a party to a treaty to ensure that its domestic law is in conformity with its international obligations is beyond doubt.[220] Where 'obligations of result' are in issue, that is, where States are required to bring about a certain situation internally, then they commonly enjoy freedom in the choice of means for implementation, although in some cases a treaty may show a preference for the adoption of legislative and/or institutional measures.

Article 2(2) of the 1966 Covenant on Civil and Political Rights calls on States to enact such 'legislative or other measures as may be necessary'[221] to give effect, among others, to article 25.[222] Words such as 'necessary' indicate that the State enjoys discretion in its choice of implementing measures, though the standard of compliance remains an international one. Just as taking the theoretically most appropriate measures of implementation is not conclusive as to the fulfilment of an international obligation, so failing to take such measures is not conclusive as to breach.[223] The variety of political and legal systems and practices of States also leads in practice to problems of interpretation and appreciation. Whether a State has fulfilled an obligation of result thus depends on a combination of factors: the initial means chosen for implementation, and the remedies available in the event that an initially incompatible situation ensues. In this context, local remedies are especially important;[224] their availability and effectiveness will often determine the question of fulfilment or breach of obligation.

---

[220] McNair, *The Law of Treaties,* (1961), 78-9; see also Brownlie, I., *Principles of Public International Law* (4th ed. 1990), 35-7; Brownlie, I., *System of the Law of Nations: State Responsibility (Part I),* (1983), 241-76; *Treatment of Polish Nationals in Danzig,* PCIJ ser. A/B no. 44 at 24; *Greco-Bulgarian Communities,* PCIJ, ser. B, no. 17, 32; *Free Zones,* PCIJ ser. A, no. 24, 12; ser. A/B, no. 46, 167; art. 27, 1969 Vienna Convention on the Law of Treaties; *Advisory Opinion, Applicability of the Obligation to Arbitrate under Section 21 of the United Nations Headquarters Agreement of 26 June 1947,* ICJ *Rep.,* 1988, 12.

[221] Art. 2(2), 1966 Covenant on Civil and Political Rights. See also, OAS Additional Protocol to the American Convention on Human Rights in the area of Economic, Social and Cultural (Protocol of San Salvador, 14 November 1988), art. 2: 'If the exercise of the rights set forth in this Protocol is not already guaranteed by legislative or other provisions, the States Parties undertake to adopt, in accordance with their constitutional processes and the provisions of this Protocol, such legislative or other measures as may be necessary for making those rights a reality': 28 *ILM* 156 (1989).

[222] Art. 25 provides: 'Every citizen shall have the right and the opportunity, without any of the distinctions mentioned in article 2 and without unreasonable restrictions: (a) To take part in the conduct of public affairs, directly or through freely chosen representatives; (b) To vote and to be elected at genuine periodic elections which shall be by universal and equal suffrage and shall be held by secret ballot, guaranteeing the free expression of the will of the electors; (c) To have access, on general terms of equality, to public service in his country.'

[223] See *Tolls on the Panama Canal* (1911-12): Hackworth, *Digest,* vi, 59 (views of the United States); *German Interests in Polish Upper Silesia* (Merits), PCIJ (1926) ser. A, no. 7, 19. The Permanent Court's reference in the *German Settlers in Poland* case to the necessity for '... equality in fact... as well as ostensible legal equality in the sense of absence of discrimination in the words of the law': PCIJ (1923) ser. B, no. 6, 24, is founded on an equivalent principle. See further *Yearbook of the ILC* (1977), ii, 23-7.

[224] The local remedies rule is firmly based in general international law, and also figures in human rights instruments; see, for example, art. 26, 1950 European Convention on Human Rights; art. 11(3), 14(7)(a), 1965 International Convention on the Elimination of All Forms of Racial Discrimination; art. 41(1)(c), 1966 Covenant on Civil and Political Rights, art. 5(2)(b), Optional Protocol thereto.

In addition to assuming obligations with regard to the individual's political rights and in regard to elections, States undertake to implement them in good faith. While they may retain choice of means among legislative incorporation, administrative regulation, informal, temporary, permanent and *ad hoc* procedures and institutions, formal measures alone will not suffice to discharge a State's responsibility.

Specific *legislative* action, prescribing the conditions for candidature, constituency delimitation, political activity and balloting, might therefore be considered a necessary condition for effective implementation. The establishment of an independent electoral commission or equivalent body may likewise be considered a further necessary condition. Whether in any given case such measures, either together or alone, are sufficient conditions for the effective attainment of free and fair elections remains to be judged in the light of the actual workings of the legal and political system as a whole.

2.5.1 Electoral commissions as 'best practice'

The importance and practical usefulness of an independent and impartial authority charged with the administration of all aspects of the electoral process are increasingly evident. That some sort of institutional mechanism is necessary is one thing, but how it should be organized and what should be its functions are other matters, essentially for local determination. The formal regulation of certain parts of the process may have priority in certain countries; for example, a central feature of recent reform in France has been the establishment of the *Commission nationale de contrôle des comptes de campagne et des financements politiques*, empowered within the context of legislative elections to propose to the *Conseil constitutionnel* that it impose the sanctions of invalidity and ineligibility.[225]

Elsewhere, national election commissions may be charged with the full range of activities: supervising and coordinating the registration of voters; holding elections; determining constituency boundaries; providing voter education; overseeing the financial aspects. Poland, for example, maintains a system of electoral institutions at national, constituency and district levels, with some variations depending on the nature of the election (Sejm, Senate or Presidential). The National Electoral Commission is a permanently functioning body charged with the task of preparing for and conducting all elections. It consists of nine judges, three each from the Supreme Court, the

---

[225] See Genevois, Bruno, 'Le nouveau rôle du juge de l'élection', in 'L'argent des élections', *Pouvoirs*, No. 70, 1994, 69; also the Belgian Loi du 4 juillet 1989 'relative a la limitation et au contrôle des dépenses électorales ainsi qu'au financement et à la comptabilité ouverte des partis politiques': *Moniteur belge, 20 juillet 1989*, 206; reports are checked by a *Commission de Contrôle* composed, according to art. 1.4, equally of members of the Chamber of Representatives and the Senate. The author is grateful to Georges Bergougnous of the *Conseil constitutionnel* for clarifying aspects of French law in this area.

Constitutional Tribunal and the Chief Administrative Court. Other Commissions are appointed for particular elections. The Constituency Electoral Commissions, for example, comprise judges from local appeal courts, while District Electoral Commissions are appointed from among the electors, by lot in the case of national referenda. The permanent duties of the National Election Commission include a general power to supervise the observance of the electoral law; the preparation and conduct of elections; co-operation with other appropriate bodies; supervising the creation and accurate maintenance of electoral registers; designing forms and stamps; drafting regulations governing the conduct of lower commissions; considering complaints about such commissions and providing them with advice and explanations; establishing and announcing the results of elections and referenda. Officials of the National Electoral Office may not belong to any political party or engage in any political activity.[226]

In its report on the November 1996 Romanian Parliamentary and Presidential Elections, the OSCE/ODIHR noted that despite the representation of competing political interests on the electoral 'bureaux' during the entire process, 'the absence of a permanent and professionally staffed Central Electoral Bureau is regarded as a major weakness... Organisation may only be improved further and the democratic process strengthened by the establishment of a permanent independent body...'[227] In the case of the Bulgarian Presidential elections, by contrast, where the political composition of the electoral commissions, at all levels, reflects the level of representation of the parties in the Parliament, ODIHR considered that the relatively high voter turnout indicated 'trust in the integrity of the electoral administration'.[228]

In established democracies, attention is also turning to the establishment or reform of electoral structures. A 1991 report in the United Kingdom strongly recommended the establishment of an election commission to take over from the massively decentralized system now managed by local authorities. Among the functions identified by the Hansard Society Commission on Electoral Campaigns were administration of elections, determination of electoral boundaries, allocation and supervision of broadcasting time, administration of election expenditure, including any state subsidies, and a role as a permanent, expert advisory body on electoral matters.[229] Accrued advantages would likely include continuity, perceived

---

[226] National Electoral Office, 'Polish Electoral Law: A Brief Outline,' paper submitted to the OSCE/ODIHR Seminar on Election Administration and Election Observation, Warsaw, 8-10 Apr. 1997.

[227] ODIHR, *Final Report,* Romanian Parliamentary and Presidential Elections, 3rd and 17th November 1996, s. 4.

[228] ODIHR, *Final Report,* Bulgarian Presidential Election, October 27 and November 3, 1996.

[229] *Agenda for Change.* The Report of the Hansard Society Commission on Election Campaigns. Hansard Society, London, 1991, 68-73.

independence, the development of in-house expertise, increased parliamentary and public access to information about electoral administration, and heightened efficiency. Drawing on the Australian and Canadian models,[230] the Hansard Society Commission also stressed the importance of independence and separate funding, qualities that have all too often been found lacking by observers of recent elections elsewhere.[231]

2.5.2 Protecting the integrity of the system

Experience confirms that an electorate is more likely to be actively engaged in political life if it has confidence in the system. This in turn may require not only an authority competent to ensure that rules and practice are followed, but also one which is itself either independent and impartial, or sufficiently representative of the competing parties.[232]

The UNTAES Electoral Code, for example, emphasizes that election officials have a special responsibility to promote a free and fair election. They are therefore required to refrain from politically influencing any voter, to perform their functions with care, competence and courtesy, to maintain strict impartiality, 'and to do nothing by way of action, attitude, manner or speech to give any other impression'. They are also forbidden from standing as candidates, from holding office in a party, or from wearing any clothing or emblem likely to be associated with a party or candidate.[233]

---

[230] Canada does not have an Election Commission as such. Rather, responsibility for federal elections and referendums has been entrusted since 1920 to one independent officer of Parliament, the Chief Electoral Officer. This Officer, who is appointed by a resolution of the House of Commons, can be removed only for cause by the Governor-General on an address by the House and the Senate. To ensure the appearance of impartiality, neither the Chief Electoral Officer nor the Assistant Chief Electoral Officer may vote in federal elections. Independence is enhanced by the authority to spend public funds voted by Parliament. The Chief Electoral Officer reports to Parliament on the activities of the Office after each election; see, for example, Elections Canada, *Thirty-fifth General Election 1993. Contributions and Expenses of Registered Political Parties and Candidates,* Ottawa, 1994; Elections Canada, *Strengthening the Foundation: Canada's Electoral System,* Annex to the Report of the Chief Electoral Officer of Canada on the 35th General Election, Ottawa, 1996.

[231] In the case of Sierra Leone, for example, the Commonwealth Observer Group found that detailed control of the electoral process in fact resided with the National Provisional Ruling Council, not the Interim National Electoral Commission, giving rise to a number of acute problems, and concluded that complete independence and greater resources would have been of immense assistance: Commonwealth Observer Group, *The Presidential and Parliamentary Elections in Sierra Leone, 26-27 February 1996,* (1996), 7-8, 28. In Tanzania, it noted that for a number of political parties, the National Electoral Commission inspired little confidence. They had not been consulted on composition, and 'the perception of a lack of neutrality and independence can only have been reinforced by the declaration of one of the original Commissioners of his intention to stand as a candidate for the (ruling party) presidential nomination'. While the Commission attempted to meet these concerns, for example, by establishing sub-committees with party representation, the lack of confidence had not been not entirely overcome by election time: Commonwealth Observer Group, *The Union Presidential and Parliamentary Elections in Tanzania, 29 October 1995,* (1996), 7.

[232] As George F. Jones, IFES Director of Programs for the Americas, put it recently, 'the critical safeguard of a free and fair election is either a random selection of voting officials, or a selection that is carefully balanced among the competing parties': 'Fraud and Corruption in Elections and Election Campaigns', Address to the Seminar on Public Ethics sponsored by the Ministry of the Interior, Republic of Argentina, Buenos Aires, 10 Dec. 1996. The use of lots in democratic government is frequently underestimated these days; see Manin, Bernard, *The Principles of Representative Government,* Cambridge University Press, 1997, ch. 1.

[233] UNTAES, Part II; below, Annexe 1.

The U.S. Center for Responsive Politics, for example, recommended the creation of an independent, non-partisan agency, insulated from political pressure and control, with the necessary resources and enforcement authority. Specific recommendations focused on the desirability of an odd-numbered commission appointed by the President (or chief executive at state level), with a bar on re-appointment; an advisory panel to recommend nominees; and appropriate restrictions on the political activity of members (in order to underline their impartiality).[234] A February 1997 forum on election law in Armenia, on the other hand, emphasised partisan participation in the selection of electoral commission membership as a key element,[235] to counter the impartiality lacking on previous occasions.[236]

The Federal Election Commission (FEC) in the United States was created in 1974 to counteract perceived abuse of the electoral system, particularly with regard to financing and expenditure limits. Many commentators consider that it has become ineffective, in part because of its bi-partisan composition.[237] As the Center for Responsive Politics observed in 1993, another problem for the FEC and similar state bodies is the fact that 'their resources, their authority and the appointment of their members are all controlled by the very persons they are supposed to regulate'.[238]

2.5.3 Preliminary conclusions

The value of independent and impartial election machinery, such as a central electoral commission and its local counterparts, obviously goes beyond that covered by a Code of Conduct. However, codes are rarely self-applying, and are likely to be most effective where administered by an authority that enjoys the confidence of the electorate. Confidence in the system may be inspired, at least initially, by ensuring equitable political representation in the commission or equivalent body, but it can also lead to weak and ineffective administration.

---

[234] See 'Enforcing the Campaign Finance Laws: An Agency Model', June 1993. Also, COGEL, 'A Model law for Campaign Finance, Ethics and Lobbying Regulation, (1991).

[235] IFES, *Europe and Asia Report,* Feb. 1997, 11.

[236] Office for Democratic Institutions and Human Rights, *Final Report,* Armenian Presidential Election, September 22, 1996.

[237] Alexander, Herbert E. & Corrado, Anthony, *Financing the 1992 Election,* M.E. Sharpe, Armonk, WY, 1995; reviewed by Sharon Steward in *The Guardian* (Journal of the Council on Governmental Ethics Laws— COGEL), Mar. 1996, 1-3.

[238] The Center for Responsive Politics, Washington, D.C., 'Enforcing the Campaign Finance Laws: An Agency Model', June 1993. Lack of independence and inadequate resources, of course, can plague any electoral administration; see Commonwealth Observer Group, *The Presidential and Parliamentary Elections in Sierra Leone, 26-27 February 1996, (1996),* 7-8, 28. Cf. Reeves, P.R., '1996 Presidential Elections in Equatorial Guinea', IFES, Mar. 1996, 43, noting that while the electoral commission benefits logistically from its close ties with the State (being effectively an office of the Ministry of the Interior), it had clearly lost credibility with opposition parties and voters precisely because of their non-existent or minimal involvement; Commonwealth Observer Group, *The Union Presidential and Parliamentary Elections in Tanzania, 29 October 1995,* (1996), 7, to similar effect.

Many States balance principal appointments by the executive with party involvement at the local level, as in Poland,[239] but practice suggests that how an electoral commission is constituted will depend very much on local circumstances, including the actual level of confidence or distrust. The model of a *permanent* institution, whose principal members are appointed on the basis of established criteria and protected against political interference, nevertheless has much to commend it.

---

[239] See also DeGregorio, P.S. & Ross, K.L., 'Albania: A Pre-Election Technical Assessment', IFES, Aug. 1996, 8-9, describing the mixed system of appointing members of the Central Election Commission, Zonal Election Commissions, and Voting Centre Election Commissions; Lansell, S.R. & Edgeworth, L.V., 'Republic of Georgia: Assessment and Voter Information Campaign, September-November 1995', IFES, Nov. 1996, Appx. D, arts. 17-31, Georgia Parliamentary Election Law; IFES, 'Republic of Moldova Presidential Elections, November 17 and December 1, 1996', ch. 1, 3, 'Law on the Election of the President of the Republic of Moldova', arts. 8-17; Klein, K., Scallan, A., Santos de Assunçao, C. & Dauphinais, D., 'Toward Credible and Legitimate Elections in Kenya: Recommendations for Action', IFES, Apr. 1996, 11-18, recommending among others that Commission membership be changed to one acceptable to political parties and NGOs, and that its independence be strengthened by the repeal of legislation allowing the Attorney-General a role in decision-making.

3. A CODE OF CONDUCT: MODEL SCOPE AND CONTENT

An almost universal, therefore probably 'natural', tendency exists on the part of humankind in competition for political power to bend every rule, and to seek every advantage in the pursuit of the vote. The strength of a Code of Conduct will lie in part perhaps in its own essentially democratic character, which results from the fact that its binding quality springs from the parties themselves, rather that from a superior legislative authority. Even though the Code may be drafted by an Electoral Commission, or ultimately be authorised by the legislature, it remains nevertheless an instrument to be subscribed to.[240] As Patrick Merloe notes,

> ... to be effective, such codes should be reached as a result of careful consultations among the parties taking part in the election, even parties that are not putting up candidates. Codes of conduct adopted mechanically from other countries are not as likely to produce positive effects on campaign behaviour.[241]

The force of a Code of Conduct as an influential tool resides further in the *reasonableness* of its content, and the extent to which it can be seen, in language comprehensible to all, to contribute to an open, free and fair discussion; in the extent to which it becomes a standard of accountability; and in the commonsensical weight it gives to the notion of responsibility for action.

The exact balance of legal rules, standards, guidelines and principles will always be a matter for local choice, taking account of time, place and circumstance, history and social and political culture. Whereas a significant measure of general agreement on the criteria for free and fair elections has been found,[242] even if at a certain level of normative generality, this is less likely in the case of a Code of Conduct; indeed, the content is even liable to

---

[240] An apparent exception may be the Code of Conduct developed in St Kitts and Nevis, prepared by a group of church organizations and the local Chamber of Commerce and Industry, but with political party input. A Committee to Promote Compliance with the Code of Conduct was also established, meeting daily in a non-partisan spirit to hear submissions about violations and to make recommendations. The Code's positive contribution may be directly related to its grassroots, popular origins. See Commonwealth Observer Group, *The General Election in St Kitts and Nevis, 3 July 1995*, (1996), 5, 12-13. A Code is only likely to be successfully 'imposed' where the authority behind it is considered credible, or enjoys credible implementing force, as was the case in Cambodia in 1993, and Bosnia and Herzegovina in 1996; see art. 1, Cambodia: Code of Conduct; art. 119, Rules and Regulations of the Provisional Election Commission (Bosnia and Herzegovina).

[241] Merloe, Patrick, 'Electoral Campaigns and Pre-Election Issues: The "Level Playing Field" and Democratic Elections', National Democratic Institute, Washington, D.C., 1994.

[242] See, for example, the Inter-Parliamentary Union, *Declaration of Criteria on Free and Fair Elections, 1994*, cited throughout this study.

change over time in the case of a single country.[243] However, there can be little doubt now of the general value of a such a code in facilitating the achievement of a free and fair election, and in promoting, consolidating and maintaining the democratic process.

The detail of many of the codes reproduced below is clearly inappropriate for inclusion in a model of general applicability; codes of conduct, by definition, will be oriented to local conditions and local experience. What may be unexceptional political activity in one context, such as motorcades, processions, loudspeakers, and so forth, may have traditionally been a cause of violent reaction in another. Equally, restrictions on critical participation in another's political meetings are likely to be seen as hindering freedom of speech and expression by activists used to the cut and thrust of political debate and the traditions of oral heckling. The fact that freedoms are restricted in this way, however, invites review in the light of what may be considered reasonably necessary in a democratic society, and of what is proportional. Previous experience, particularly a history of violent incidents, may justify some limitations on political rights and freedoms. A balance will always need to be struck, however, between the objectives of a peaceful campaign and the effective implementation of political rights at individual and party level. The risk is, and recent experience suggests that this is a real concern, that political debate will be stifled, political issues will not be addressed, and the electorate will consequently remain uninformed and thus practically unable to make a rational choice between competing options.

The Commonwealth Observer Group found that the Code of Conduct applied in the 1996 Bangladesh elections 'proved to be highly effective in regulating the conduct of political parties and candidates', and helped to ensure that the political parties and candidates for the most part conducted themselves responsibly. The strict guidelines aimed 'to ensure that each political party started from the same footing and that size and influence, whether financial or otherwise would have little or no effect'. In contrast to earlier elections, there were no hoardings, decorated arches, huge banners, or defacement of posters; the use of motorised vehicles for campaigning was prohibited; and campaigners were limited in the use of microphones. If one consequence was a 'low-key' campaign, another was the increased resort to door-to-door canvassing.[244] In Pakistan also, the Commonwealth Observer Group noted that the campaign was muted by the effect of new restrictions

---

[243]   Compare the Codes of Conduct promulgated in Bangladesh in 1991 and 1996; below, Annexes 4 and 15.

[244]   Commonwealth Observer Group, *The Parliamentary Elections in Bangladesh, 12 June 1996,* (1997), 12, 14, 26. It was recommended that the system of Electoral Enquiry Committees might be strengthened, that more be done to remove all forms of party influence from the polling centre, and that increased penalties for breach of election laws and the Code of Conduct be considered, for example, in the form of summary and expeditious action against offenders: ibid., 26.

grouped under the Code of Conduct, limiting processions, election camps, and the use of posters, banners, loudspeakers; here, too, a return to door-to-door campaigning was in evidence.[245]

In other cases, one frequent goal of an agreed Code of Conduct — closer co-operation between competing parties — in fact came first. In Sierra Leone, such co-operation helped free the campaign of violence and intimidation, and that in turn was facilitated by an informal grouping, the All Political Parties Association (APPA). This brought the parties together,[246] and enabled them to agree on a *de facto* Code of Conduct.[247] A similar development occurred in Ghana in 1996, where the Inter-Party Advisory Committee (IPAC) acted as a non-statutory advisory body to the Electoral Commission. It met first monthly and then more frequently, and provided the Electoral Commission the chance to disseminate information uniformly to the parties and solicit advice concerning electoral administration. As in Cambodia in 1993, the meetings also provided the parties with an opportunity to express their concerns and views on a variety of election-related issues, adding to the transparency of the administration.[248]

The integrity of the electoral process depends as much on public perceptions of *fairness* and *decency,* as on *openness* and *accountability*. Democratic elections are too important to be left to 'form' alone. They require 'a climate of equitable implementation', which may be developed in turn through the complementary impact of laws and Codes of Conduct. Some areas and issues are clearly governable by rules, while others lend themselves more to regulation or resolution through the application of more general guidelines, either on the basis of self-regulation, or through an intermediary body.

3.1 The potential scope of a Code of Conduct

Patrick Merloe has suggested that, with regard to political parties, Codes of Conduct might usefully address issues such as not interfering in the campaign activities of other political contestants; enforcing party discipline to prevent violence and intimidation; respecting the rights of voters and other contestants; and refraining from negative campaigning. They can also make affirmative points, for example, by stressing ballot secrecy, or emphasizing the duty to accept the results of valid elections.[249] So far as they might help to

---

[245] Commonwealth Observer Group, *The General Election in Pakistan, 3 February 1997*, (1997), 20-22.

[246] There was one exception, the National Unity Party, which was perceived as the Government's creation; in time, however, it too was brought in.

[247] Commonwealth Observer Group, *The Presidential and Parliamentary Elections in Sierra Leone, 26-27 February 1996*, (1996), 19.

[248] Statement of the National Democratic Institute for International Affairs (NDI), Pre-Election Assessment Delegation, Accra, 19 Nov. 1996.

[249] Merloe, Patrick, 'Electoral Campaigns and Pre-Election Issues: The "Level Playing Field" and Democratic Elections', National Democratic Institute, Washington, D.C., 1994.

create or maintain a 'level playing field', Codes of Conduct can contribute to public confidence by promoting an electoral process that is administratively correct and free from the perception of partisanship; that is open and transparent; involves all the participants; is accessible to observers; and which promotes respect for the vote.[250]

Additionally, there may be some scope for a Code of Conduct to influence party structure and behaviour, for example, in the matter of candidature. In many systems, either formally or informally, party membership or endorsement by a party is an essential pre-condition to exercise of the right to stand for election. In several countries today, parties are wrestling with the challenge of increasing the participation of women or minorities,[251] while in others the question of formal *disqualification* is currently controversial, in regard both to individuals[252] and to types and categories of parties.[253] At a certain point, ideology and the right of everyone to participate in public life sit uncomfortably together; a Code of Conduct, located within the electoral system overall, may thus help to promote reasonable opportunities for anyone to offer themselves as a candidate for election.

---

[250] Merloe, Patrick, 'Electoral Operations, Human Rights and Public Confidence in a Democratic System', National Democratic Institute, Washington, D.C., 1994.

[251] See, among others, Gallagher M. & Marsh, M., eds., *Candidate Selection in Comparative Perspective. The Secret Garden of Politics,* Sage Modern Politics Series, vol. 18, (1988); Nicholson, B., 'From interest group to (almost) equal citizenship: Women's representation in the Norwegian Parliament', 46 *Parliamentary Affairs* 254 (1993); Inter-Parliamentary Union, Specialized Inter-Parliamentary Conference, 'Towards Partnership between Men and Women in Politics', New Delhi, 14-18 Feb. 1997, Concluding Statement by the President on the Outcome of the Conference.

[252] On disqualification see, for example, DeGregorio, P.S. & Ross, K.L., 'Albania: A Pre-Election Technical Assessment', IFES, Aug. 1996, 5-7, describing the work of the 'Verification Commission' which determines whether potential candidates were involved in so-called genocide activities before 1991, and whose certification is a prerequisite for participation in the election; Human Rights Watch, 'Leaving Human Rights Behind: The Context of the Presidential Elections', 16 May 1997, noting with regard to Iran that while there is a real contest *within* the clerical leadership, 'all candidates representing opposition viewpoints have been arbitrarily disqualified by the Council of Guardians', which has broad powers to bar candidates and annul election results. Compare *Gitonas and Others v. Greece* (1 July 1997), in which the European Court of Human Rights held unanimously that there was no breach of article 3, Protocol 1 of the European Convention on Human Rights, when the election of five MPs was annulled by reason of their having held public office during the preceding three years. Such disqualifications, said the Court, served the dual purpose of ensuring that candidates of different political persuasions enjoyed equal means of influence (since public office holders may on occasion have an unfair advantage over other candidates); and protecting the electorate from pressure from such officials.

[253] Art. 4, Constitution of France, provides that political parties, 'doivent respecter les principes de la souveraineté nationale et de la démocratie'. Art. 71 of the 1995 Uganda Constitution, for example, sets out criteria for the formation and existence of political parties; they must have a 'national character', not be based on gender, ethnic origin, religious belief or 'other section division', must be organized in conformity with the democratic principles in the Constitution, must themselves conduct regular elections in a democratic manner, and account for their funding sources: Cooper, L. & Henderson, J., 'Uganda: A Pre-Election Assessment Report', Jan. 1996, 22-3. See also, Human Rights Watch, 'Algeria-Elections in the Shadow of Violence and Repression,' 20 May 1997, highlighting, among others, restrictions on the categories of parties (prohibited where based on religion, region, language or gender).

3.2 The potential content of a Code of Conduct

Everyone has the right to participate in public life, to vote in periodic elections by secret ballot and on the basis of universal suffrage. These rights, clearly established in international law, will only be effective where they are respected, where voters are able to make an informed choice, and where the electoral environment is free from violence and intimidation and the electoral process from partiality. The right to take part in public life depends also for its effectiveness on fairness, including a balance between contestants in their capacity to present their policies and programmes and campaign practices which inform the electorate and highlight issues, not irrelevancies.

A Code of Conduct can promote standards by providing guidance to those who seek election, who manage the process or report the campaign, and a yardstick by which to measure their performance. A Code of Conduct can also set out, and thereby raise, the expectations of the electorate in relation to official, party and personal accountability. It can help to counter natural or contrived inequalities among contestants, and the often distorting influence of money.

Whether 'legislated' by an electoral commission or the product of an agreement between the parties, the *authority* of a Code of Conduct will vary. It is likely to be greatest where there is confidence in the electoral administration itself, or where confidence emerges between parties, contestants and administrators. Negotiating or mediating a Code of Conduct can thus itself contribute to the creation of a climate of equitable implementation and responsible campaigning. Equally, the constraining effect of such a Code will be a social and political variable; so far as violation of its terms disappoints public expectations, it is in practice likely to lead not so much to penalties or annulment (which will generally remain the options for breach of the law itself), as to a refusal to accept the results at the local level (with all its attendant dangers for public order), and to a refusal by external observers to 'certify' the election as free and fair.

Drawing on the experience described above and on examples such as those reproduced in the annexes below, and while recognizing the critical importance of an autochthonous solution, the following Model Code of Conduct for Elections therefore aims to highlight the principal issues and categories. It acknowledges that a successful and informed electoral process is the joint responsibility of all involved: political parties and candidates; supporters and voters; police and security forces; governments and public officials; media and observers. The objectives of the Model are nevertheless quite straightforward: (1) To propose a minimum standard of good electoral practice, combining elements of law and experience; and (2) to provide a basis upon which governments, election administration bodies, political parties and candidates can better co-operate in the promotion of peaceful and informed elections.

A MODEL CODE OF CONDUCT FOR ELECTIONS

1. RULE OF LAW

All political parties and candidates should accept the authority of the national election commission or other competent body, and should implement and abide by all such laws, rules and regulations as govern the holding of elections.

All political parties and candidates should facilitate the access of national election commission officials and registered observers to all their public political meetings and other electoral activities.

1.1 Corrupt practices

No political party, candidate, agent or supporter should offer any bribe, inducement or reward to voters, make any threat of retaliation or reprisal to voters or other participants in an election, offer any gift for the purpose of inducing another to stand or not to stand for election, or intimidate or impersonate voters.

No political party, candidate, agent or supporter should seek the support of any public official or official of the national election commission or other competent body in order to promote or hinder the election of any candidate.

The interests of government and party should be clearly distinguished. In particular, members of the governing party should not use government funds or resources for the purposes of electioneering otherwise than on a basis of equality with other contestants.

1.2 Responsibilities

It is the responsibility of all political parties and candidates to ensure that the Code of Conduct is strictly observed by their representatives, campaign workers and active supporters.

All political parties and candidates shall be vocal against violence.

It is the responsibility of the police to maintain public order. In carrying out their duties, the police and other security agencies should act impartially and with due regard to the rights of all participants in the election. Permits required for meetings, processions or other political activities should be issued without discrimination and on a basis of equality for all.

Political parties and candidates should co-operate with law enforcement agencies in promoting a peaceful election environment and in protecting the security and integrity of the democratic process.

In the case of public disturbances or breaches of the election law or Code of Conduct, political parties, candidates, agents and supporters should advise and seek the assistance of the police and other authorities concerned, and in no case resort to measures of their own.

All political parties and candidates should respect the rights of others and should take all necessary and reasonable steps to conduct their campaigns in a peaceful environment.

2.   POLITICAL PARTIES AND FUNDING

Recognizing that financial issues can distort the electoral process, leading to a lack of public confidence, political parties should consider themselves bound by the principles of transparency and disclosure. In addition to publicising their constitution and aims, political parties should disclose their income and assets, sources of income, and expenses.

Where necessary to establish or re-establish equality between the parties, and in order to encourage the widest dissemination of views, governments should consider providing financial assistance for the conduct of election campaigns and such other measures as may contribute to a fair and informed electoral process.

3.   POLITICAL PARTIES AND CANDIDATES

Recognising the value of information and co-operation in promoting the confidence of the electorate, political parties and candidates should establish effective means of contact and communication between themselves, with a view to discussing matters of concern and avoiding conflict.

Political parties and candidates should instruct their agents and supporters to observe the electoral law and the Code of Conduct, and take the necessary steps to ensure compliance.

Every candidate should act in good faith and with integrity in matters of speech and conduct.

Political parties should contribute to the education of voters in the manner of marking the ballot paper and casting votes.

4.   POLITICAL PARTIES AND CANDIDATURE

In so far as the creation and registration of political parties may be regulated by legislation, the law should allow for the broadest possible representation of different views and permit only such reasonable restrictions as are necessary in a democratic society.

The electoral system and, where appropriate, the criteria for membership of political parties, should take into account of the right of everyone to participate in public life and provide a reasonable opportunity for anyone to offer themselves as a candidate for election.

5. CAMPAIGN ACTIVITY AND FAIR CAMPAIGN PRACTICES

5.1 Peace and public order

Arms, other dangerous weapons, firecrackers and explosives shall not be allowed in public meetings.

Political parties and candidates should ensure that their campaign activity does not incite violence, aggravate sectional differences, create mutual hatred, or cause tension between different groups or communities. Abusive, inflammatory or indecent language should be avoided, and all the necessary steps should be taken in good faith to avoid violent confrontation.

Political parties, candidates, agents and supporters should not obstruct or break up meetings organized by other parties and candidates, prevent the distribution of handbills and leaflets, or interfere with other parties' political material, for example, by defacement or over-postering. It is the responsibility of political parties and candidates to ensure that their supporters do not engage in activities likely to lead to a breach of the peace.

5.2 Meetings and processions

In order to minimize disorder and confrontation, the organizers of public political meetings, marches, processions or demonstrations, should advise the police or other competent authority, as well as other parties contesting the election, of the intended time, date and place. They should comply with such regulations or directions as may be made for the maintenance of public order and the movement of traffic.

In the event that two or more parties propose to organize simultaneous processions or demonstrations, they should establish contact with one another with a view to resolving the conflict peaceably, seeking the mediation of an appropriate third party wherever necessary.

5.3 Fair campaign practices

Political parties, candidates and supporters should,

■ recognize the freedom of all to campaign for election, to access potential voters, to disseminate their views, to hold public meetings, to access the media, to canvass freely for members and support, and to publish and distribute notices and election materials;

- avoid criticism of other political parties, their leaders and candidates that has no bearing on their public activities, or that is based on unverified allegations or distortion. Criticism and comments should be confined to issues, policies, programmes, and past record, and should respect the right of others to hold their own opinions;

- refrain from any criticism of the private life of party leaders, candidates and workers that is unrelated to their public activities, and from any abuse of campaigners for reasons of race, religion, gender, social origins, background or any other reason;

- respect the individual's rights, refrain from demonstrating outside or picketing an individual's house, and ensure that property is only used for election purposes with the permission of the owner;

- respect the freedom of the press and not harass or obstruct the work of journalists;

- respect such legal limits as may be laid down with regard to electoral expenses, the time for campaign activity, wall-writing, the use of banners, posters, bulletin boards, microphones and loudspeaker equipment;

- respect such regulations as may govern political advertising and access to the media, including newspapers, television and radio.

Candidates should assume responsibility for the work of their campaign staff and supporters; all campaign material should be expressly approved by the candidate, or carry a disclaimer indicating that it was not so approved

Candidates should commit themselves not only to compliance with election laws, but also to campaign standards of decency and fairness.

6.   THE MEDIA

It is the responsibility of the media, as servants of the public interest, to report honestly and impartially on the events of the election campaign, to ensure that news stories are accurate, to distinguish editorial and commentary clearly from reporting, and to avoid either sensational or trivializing language.

When presenting controversial issues, it is the responsibility of the media to provide fair representation of opposing sides.

State-owned media, in particular, should ensure impartiality in its reporting of electoral activities and equality of availability for the dissemination of political programmes.

As a contribution to the dissemination of ideas and the promotion of an informed choice by the electorate, the media should accord access to eligible political parties on an equal basis. Political advertising in the media should be guaranteed to all parties equally and available at the lowest price.

The media may reject political material only where it is not in good taste, or where it is contrary to the public interest and security, and subject to the provision of reasons and an opportunity to make the necessary changes.

In presenting political material to the public, the media should ensure that it is accompanied by the appropriate disclaimer or explanation.

Like political parties and candidates, the media are responsible for ensuring compliance with the election laws and guidelines.

The media should rectify, promptly and with due prominence, any inaccuracies, ensure appropriate correction and apologies, and afford a right of reply.

The media should exercise special care in publishing the results of opinion polls. In particular, the media should ensure that the sponsors, organizers and funding of opinion polls are identified, and that methodology and sampling are clearly described.

Members of the media should,

- conduct themselves in accordance with the highest standards of professionalism, defend freedom of information at all times, and avoid distortion, suppression, falsification, misrepresentation and censorship;
- not accept bribes or any other inducement that might influence the exercise of their professional responsibilities;
- always avoid language which encourages discrimination, ridicule, prejudice or hatred.

In order to promote public confidence, appropriate measures should be taken to monitor access to the media and its performance with regard to election campaigns.

7. ELECTION ADMINISTRATION AND POLLING

7.1 Election administration

Elections should be organized and administered by independent, impartial and trained officials, within a national election commission or other competent institution. Election administrators should be free from interference by government or parties, and should be provided with sufficient funds to allow them to fulfil their responsibilities. The principles of openness and accountability, transparency and disclosure, apply equally to the electoral administration as to political parties and candidates.

It should be the responsibility of the national election commission or other competent electoral authority to provide for constituency delimitation, following consultation with parties and the electorate.

The national election commission or other competent electoral authority should encourage and facilitate the registration of all eligible to vote and that no eligible elector is denied the right to vote, for example, by way of intimidation or the misuse of relief or other benefits.

The secrecy of the ballot shall be maintained at all times. The national election commission or other competent electoral authority should take all necessary steps to ensure that secrecy is preserved, whether at the moment of voting, counting, or through the analysis of trends, for example, in small voting units.

In appropriate circumstances, the national election commission or other competent electoral authority may be authorised to certify the entitlement of political parties to media privileges or other electoral rights.

7.2 Co-operation

Political parties and candidates should co-operate with election administration officials in facilitating the registration of voters and in verifying and correcting electoral rolls.

Political parties and candidates should co-operate with election administration officials in order to ensure a smooth and peaceful ballot. They should ensure that authorised party workers are identified.

Political parties, candidates, agents and supporters should co-operate with election officials in facilitating all stages of voting, counting, and the announcement of results.

7.3 Polling day

In the conduct of voting, a balance should be struck between the prevention of interference and intimidation, on the one hand, and an open, visible process, on the other hand. Only voters, election administration officials, accredited observers, including representatives of the parties and the media, should be permitted access to any polling station.

Special provision should be made to enable handicapped or illiterate voters to exercise their right to vote by secret ballot.

No campaign material should be permitted in any polling station, and no campaign activity should be conducted on polling day, either at all where prohibited by law or within such distance of any polling station as may be prescribed by law.

Military or other personnel responsible for security at polling stations should ensure that their presence does not interfere with the right of voters to vote freely and in secret.

7.4 Domestic observers

Subject only to reasonable regulation by the national election commission or other competent electoral authority, elections should be open to domestic observation by citizens, parties, media and concerned organizations, as an aspect of the basic right to participate in public life.

The national election commission or other competent electoral authority should ensure that election observers are accredited and provided with the appropriate documentation.

All stages of the electoral process should be open to observation, including registration of electors, the campaign, the operation of polling stations during polling, the operation of the count in each polling station and the totalling and scrutiny (including the determination of claims made by candidates or their representatives) at each level.

In order to fulfil their role, observers should enjoy freedom of movement, the freedom to receive and communicate information, and access to relevant premises and documents. Any accredited observer is free to have contact with any person at any time and anywhere and to attend all election related events.

Observers should not interfere with any stage of the ballot. Observers may accept complaints from candidates and should refer them to the competent election administration officials.

7.5 International observers

Elections may also be open to international observation, in accordance with accepted international standards and with the general provisions relating to domestic observers.

International observers may include representatives of governments and international organizations, parliamentarians, representatives of international non-governmental organizations, or individuals. All bodies sending observers should be free in their choice of observers.

International observers should maintain a position of neutrality in the election process and in relation to national authorities, parties and candidates, voters, press and media.

International observers should consider themselves bound by the principles of transparency and disclosure, and avoid any or any appearance of a conflict of interest during their presence at an election.

International observers should comply at all times with national law and the Code of Conduct.

International observers should base their conclusions on verifiable, factual evidence, and apply international standards in assessing the outcome of an election.

7.6 Dispute resolution

The national election commission or other competent electoral authority should provide impartial, expeditious and efficient means for the resolution of disputes and irregularities in the campaign and in the administration of the election. The necessary steps should be taken to ensure that dispute resolution procedures are known to all participants in the election.

Political parties, candidates and others should not abuse the complaints procedure.

8.   RESULTS

All political parties, candidates, agents and supporters should accept the outcome of an election conducted in accordance with the law and should accept the authority of the constitutionally established government.

Annexes

Codes of Conduct for Elections

Annexes

1. Code of Conduct for Elections in the Region under the United Nations Transitional Administration in Eastern Slavonia, Baranja and Western Sirmium (UNTAES) 77

2. Liberia: Special Elections Code of Conduct 1997 87

3. Pakistan: Code of Conduct for the Political Parties and Contesting Candidates, General Elections 1997 89

4. Bangladesh: Code of Conduct for Elections 1996 93

5. Bosnia and Herzegovina: OSCE—Rules and Regulations of the Provisional Election Commission 1996 95

    Electoral Code of Conduct for Political Parties, Candidates and Election Workers 95

    Regulations Concerning the Obligations of Governments in Relation to the Media in Bosnia and Herzegovina 96

    Standards of Professional Conduct for the Media and Journalists 97

    Media Experts Commission (Extracts) 98

    Rules And Regulations For International Election Observers 99

6. India: Model Code of Conduct 1996 101

7. St. Kitts and Nevis: Code of Conduct for the Political Process 1995 105

8. United Republic of Tanzania: Guidelines 1995 108

    Guidelines for Government Owned Media During Election Campaign 108

    Guidelines for the Private News Media 110

9. Palestine: Declaration of Principles on Interim Self-Government Arrangements, Annex II, Protocol concerning Elections, 1993 112

10. Panama: Commitment of Santa Maria La Antigua, Ethical Electoral Commitment, 'Justice and Peace' Commission, Panama, September 1993 120

11. Cambodia: Code of Conduct 1993 122

12. Ghana: Code of Conduct for Political Parties for Public
    Elections 1992   124

13. Guyana: Guidelines for Media and Political Parties 1992 ..   126

14. Seychelles: Code of Conduct to be Adhered to by Political
    Parties, their Members and Supporters on an Election or
    Referendum 1992   129

15. Bangladesh: Code of Conduct to be adhered to by Political
    Parties 1991   132

16. OSCE: Election Observation Code Of Conduct   134

ANNEX 1:

CODE OF CONDUCT FOR ELECTIONS IN THE REGION UNDER THE UNITED NATIONS TRANSITIONAL ADMINISTRATION IN EASTERN SLAVONIA, BARANJA AND WESTERN SIRMIUM (UNTAES)[254]

Preamble

Considering the specific circumstances under which the elections are to be held,

Bearing in mind the relevant legislation of the Republic of Croatia and the respective international instruments and obligations,

Upon mutual agreement of those concerned, the Transitional Administrator (hereinafter the 'TA'), under his authority deriving from the Basic Agreement on the Region of Eastern Slavonia, Baranja and Western Sirmium (S/1995/951) and United Nations Security Council Resolution 1037 (hereinafter 'SCR 1037(1996)'), promulgates this Code of Conduct for election of members of representative bodies of local self-government and local administration and self-government units in Eastern Slavonia, Baranja and Western Sirmium (hereinafter referred to in this Code as the 'Region'):

PART I

Political Parties, Party Members, Candidates and their Sympathizers

1.   All registered political parties, party members, candidates and their sympathizers shall promote conditions conducive to the conduct of free and fair elections, and a climate of democratic tolerance in which political activity may take place without fear of coercion, intimidation or reprisals.

2.   All registered political parties and candidates must actively encourage their members and sympathizers to comply with all the provisions of this Code. Parties and candidates will discipline and restrain their party office-bearers, employees, candidates, members and sympathizers from committing any violation of Croatian electoral legislation and of the rules and procedures established by the Joint Implementation Committee on Elections (hereinafter referred to as the 'JIC'), including the present Code of Conduct.

3.   All registered political parties and candidates must acknowledge the authority of the TA under SCR 1037, through the JIC, to organize the elections, to assist in their conduct and to certify the results. Registered parties and candidates shall:

a)   Carry out and abide by the rules and procedures established by the JIC;

b)   Facilitate the access of members of the JIC election officials and election monitors to all political meetings and other electoral activities;

---

[254]   Published under the authority of the Transitional Administrator, UNTAES Public Affairs, Vukovar, Apr. 1997.

c) Take all possible steps to ensure the safety of members of the JIC, election officials and election monitors from exposure to insult, hazard or threat during their official duties;

d) Ensure the attendance and participation of members of the JIC, election officials and election monitors at meetings of any party liaison committee and other forums convened by or on behalf of the JIC.

4. All registered political parties, political party members, candidates and sympathizers commit themselves to:

a) Promote free and fair elections;

b) Encourage the free expression of the will of the electors;

c) Publicly condemn violence and intimidation:

d) Reject any form of discrimination based on race, gender, ethnicity, language, class, or religion in connection with the elections and political activity;

e) Give wide publicity to this Code;

f) Promote accurate information on the electoral processes for these elections.

5. Registered political parties and candidates shall not engage in practices that are corrupt or violate the integrity of the electoral process, such as, but not limited to bribery of voters, intimidation of voters, and inducing a person to vote knowing that person is not qualified to vote.

6. All registered political parties and candidates must promote an atmosphere in which elections can be conducted in a manner that is fair, both during the campaign period and on polling day. On polling day, parties and candidates must respect the secrecy and integrity of the ballot. They must cooperate with election officials to ensure peaceful and orderly polling and complete freedom for the voters to exercise their franchise without being subject to any annoyance, disturbance or intimidation.

7. All registered political parties and candidates have the right to present their political principles and ideas without intimidation or threat. However, parties and candidates shall not create an atmosphere that leads to intimidation and harassment by behaving in such a way that could incite violence. Parties and candidates shall avoid publishing false, inflammatory or defamatory allegations about the personal conduct of another party or candidate.

8. Subject to the approval. of the TA, all registered political parties and candidates have the right to hold public meetings, rallies, marches and other similar public events as long as they are conducted in an atmosphere that is peaceful. Written notification must be given to the United Nations Transitional Authority in Eastern Slavonia, Baranja and Western Sirmium (hereinafter referred to as 'UNTAES') Electoral Unit at least 72 hours before a meeting, rally, march or other similar public event is scheduled to be held. The UNTAES Electoral Unit will then notify the local station commander of the Transitional Police Force. Political Parties and candidates will not be granted approval to hold public meetings if previous and present circumstances indicate that there will be a threat to public order, public health or the safety of people and property. Political parties and candidates will not be granted approval to hold such events simultaneously or in close proximity to

similar political events organized by other parties or candidates. It is strictly forbidden to carry or display arms, weapons or materials that may be used as weapons at political meetings, rallies, marches, demonstrations, polling stations and during any gathering of a political nature.

9.   All registered political parties and candidates must respect the right of other parties and candidates to conduct their campaign in a peaceful environment and have access to and canvass support from potential voters without fear of reprisals. Political parties and candidates must not use or incite others to use violence or intimidation against other parties, candidates or their sympathizers.

10. Any registered political party, candidate, national association, international organisation or individual has the right to lodge a complaint about the electoral process with the Local Election Commission (hereinafter referred to as the 'LEC') and the appropriate UNTAES Election Field Office. The LEC, with the assistance of the UNTAES Election Field Office, will endeavour to resolve complaints informally. All complaints that relate to either serious violations of the rules and procedure established by the JIC or violations of Croatian electoral legislation will be submitted to the UNTAES Electoral Unit in Vukovar, which will arrange for the complaint to be adjudicated by the Elections Appeals Commission (hereinafter referred to as the 'EAC'). The EAC will issue opinions with appropriate recommendations to the TA, through the JIC. Parties, candidates, national associations, international organisations and individuals must not abuse the right to complain by making false, frivolous or vexatious complaints.

11. All registered political parties and candidates must not convene or hold public political activity in the Region after midnight, 24 house before the day for elections, until closing of the polling stations on election day. They must not make use of radio, television or newspaper after midnight, 24 hours before the day for the elections, for promoting or opposing a particular registered political party or the election of a particular candidate.

12. All registered political parties and candidates must reassure sympathizers and voters about the impartiality of the JIC, the secrecy and integrity of the ballot and of the vote.

13. Although registered political parties and candidates may file complaints regarding the electoral process, once all complaints have been resolved or adjudicated, all registered political par-ties and candidates must accept the result of the elections after they have been certified by the TA.

PART II

Election Officials

1.   This part of the Code shall apply to all election officials involved in implementing elections in the Region, including those working for UNTAES.

2.   In performing their tasks under this Code, UNTAES election officials and electoral bodies shall take due account of Croatian legislation on the conduct of

elections, including, where applicable, election verification rules and procedures. Nothing in this Code derogates or modifies in any way the authority of the TA as set out in, *inter alia,* SCR 1037 (1996).

3.   All election officials must promote conditions conducive to the conduct of free and fair elections in which the secrecy and integrity of the ballot are respected. All election officials undertake to:

a)   Refrain from politically influencing any voter;

b)   Perform all duties and functions with care, competence and courtesy;

c)   Maintain strict impartiality in carrying out duties and functions and to do nothing by way of action, attitude, manner or speech to give any other impression;

d)   Reject and dissociate themselves from any intimidation, force, sexual harassment, hostility, injury, disadvantage or threat of reprisal to any person or damage to any property that may disrupt or influence the process or result of the elections.

e)   Reject and object to any form of discrimination based on race. gender, ethnicity, language, class or religion in connection with the elections and political activity.

4.   Injection officials shall not commit or attempt any act of corruption. Such acts will include the commission or omission of an act in the performance of or in connection with one's duties in exchange for money, gift or promise of reward from any candidates, registered political party, or any representative or agent of a candidate or party. Election officials shall make every effort to oppose or combat any act of corruption that is discovered in the course of their duties.

5.   Election officials shall make every effort to attend meetings, training classes or workshops that are set up to facilitate the carrying out of their functions.

6.   All election officials must accept the authority of the JIC for the conduct of elections and must not impede access of its members in carrying out their official functions.

7.   All election officials must accept the role of duly appointed representatives of registered political parties and candidates and their right to object to irregular procedures.

8.   During the election period, election officials are forbidden to stand as candidates or be included on a party list for the elections, work for or be paid by any party or candidate in connection with the elections, be the holder of an office in a party, or wear any apparel or emblem likely to be associated with any party or candidate.

9.   All election officials must provide UNTAES staff with all necessary assistance in carrying out their duties and must actively assist with voter education campaigns. They must not impede political parties from freely conducting their campaigns. All election officials must maintain the integrity and secrecy of the ballot at all times and must not interfere directly or indirectly with the free exercise of the electoral right of a person. They must safeguard all election material entrusted to them and assist all observers, monitors and supervisors in carrying out their duties.

PART III
The Media

Section I

Media Coverage of the Elections

1.   Local authorities and the media throughout Croatia must promote conditions which provide for freedom of the media, fair, accurate and unbiased media coverage and which safeguard against political censorship, unfair advantage and unequal access to the media for registered political parties and candidates during the elections.

2.   Under his authority to certify the elections, the TA will take into consideration media coverage of the elections as a contributing factor towards free and fair elections.

3.   Local authorities and UNTAES must ensure that journalists and other members of the press, who are either from the Region or outside the Region, enjoy freedom of movement and unhindered pursuit of their professional activities while covering elections for the Region. They shall not be subjected to detention, harassment or interference of any kind in pursuit of their legitimate professional activities.

4.   There shall be no censorship of freedom of information about parties, candidates and the electoral process. There shall be no sanctions or penalties on journalists, editors, publications and broadcasting stations for opinions expressed about the parties, candidates and the electoral process unless such expression constitutes or promotes incitement to hatred or violence.

5.   Local authorities and UNTAES will allow the media to have access to the public to investigate and present information on the elections.

6.   The media throughout Croatia must ensure equitable access to the media for all registered political parties and candidates competing for elections in the Region. Such access will include access to commercial presentations and news coverage with respect to print space, amount of time allotted for coverage, fairness in placement or timing and other appropriate measures.

7.   The media must seek to ensure that information reported is factually accurate, complete, fair and unbiased. They must make a clear distinction between factual reporting and editorial comment and avoid distortion, suppression, falsification, misrepresentation and censorship. Additionally, journalists, editors, publications and broadcasting stations have an obligation to rectify any inaccuracies promptly with due prominence, ensure appropriate correction and apologies and afford the right of reply.

8.   Although criticism of political parties and candidates must be expected during any electoral campaign, the media must avoid language which encourages racial, ethnic or religious hatred or that constitutes incitement to discrimination, ridicule, prejudice, violence or hatred.

9.   The media must avoid promoting parties and candidates encouraging violence or hatred or which make false, inflammatory or defamatory allegations about the personal conduct of another party or candidate.

10. The media must maintain the highest professional and ethical standards at all times. They must not accept bribes or any other inducement that might influence the exercise of their professional responsibilities. They must endeavour to protect sources of information.

Section 2

Monitoring of the Media

1. The Media Experts Commission (hereinafter referred to as the 'MEC') is established by the JIC as an advisory body to the JIC to ensure that registered political parties, candidates and the media fulfil their obligations in relation to coverage of the elections as outlined in the present Code. The MEC will exercise its functions through the JIC.

2. No later than five days after election day, the MEC will submit a final report to the JIC and to the TA with an assessment of the media coverage of the elections and the impact of such coverage on free and fair elections.

3. Members of the MEC will serve in their personal capacity. The MEC shall be composed of:

a) A Chair, appointed by the JIC;

b) One member appointed by the Government of the Republic of Croatia and one appointed by the local Serb community;

c) Two journalists appointed by the JIC, one from inside the Region and another from outside the Region;

d) One member appointed by the Organisation for Security and Cooperation in Europe to act as an observer;

e) A member appointed by UNTAES.

4. The MEC will be served by UNTAES. It will meet regularly in UNTAES Headquarters in Vukovar. The MEC may meet at a place other than Vukovar, if the Chair deems it necessary to facilitate its proceedings.

5. Any recommendation made by the MEC will be based on the consensus of its members. In the event that a consensus cannot be reached and this results in a tie, the Chair will break the tie.

6. The MEC will advise the JIC and make recommendations on procedural aspects relating to coverage of the elections by the media, including recommendations on resolution of problems. The duties of the MEC will be to promote and monitor:

a) Issuance of accreditation to foreign journalists for the Region;

b) Equitable access to the media for all registered political parties and candidates. A detailed schedule will be drawn up in consultation with the media to allot equal broadcast time and print space to all registered political parties and candidates;

c) The fulfilment of obligations of the local authorities and UNTAES to ensure security of journalists and the unhindered pursuit of their professional activities;

d) The performance of the media in providing fair and accurate coverage, as well as equitable access for all registered political parties and candidates.

7.   The MEC will intervene to informally resolve all problems encountered in the course of its work. If the problem cannot be resolved, it will be referred to the JIC.

8.   The MEC will refer to the JIC all problems which constitute serious violations of Croatian electoral legislation, the present Code of Conduct and other rules and procedures established by the JIC. The MEC will provide the JIC with a description of the problem, any action taken and, if appropriate, a recommendation on how to resolve the problem. Such recommendations may include the issuance of retractions and/or apologies and the withdrawal of privileges. Depending on the nature of the problem, the JIC may resolve the problem, refer it to the TA, or have it adjudicated by the EAC.

PART IV

Protection of Electoral Rights

Section 1

Right to Lodge Complaints

1.   Complaints can be submitted by

a)   UNTAES Election Field Offices,

b)   Election Commissions,

c)   Registered Political Parties,

d)   Candidates,

e)   National Associations and International Organisations,

f)   Individuals.

Section 2

Procedure For Lodging Complaints

1.   Complaints must first be submitted to the LEC and to the UNTAES Election Field Office.

2.   In exercising their powers and performing their duties under this Code and other relevant instruments, UNTAES election officials and electoral bodies shall endeavour to fully co-operate and co-ordinate their activities with respective authorised Croatian bodies, including the Electoral Commission of the Republic of Croatia and the Constitutional Court of the Republic of Croatia.

3.   Complaints regarding irregularities in the nomination procedure, the campaign, voting, counting and the election must be submitted within 48 hours from the date of the:

a)   Alleged violation which constitutes the basis for the complaint or

b)   Receipt of the written evidence to which the complaint relates.

4.   Complaints must be made in writing, signed by or on behalf of the complainant. Every complaint must include:

a)   Name, address and, if possible, telephone numbers of the complainant;

b)   Full and complete statement of the nature and all details of the complaint;

c)   Full and complete description of all relevant evidence relied upon by the complainant in support of the complaint;

d)   Names, addresses and telephone numbers, if applicable, of all relevant witnesses who may be relied upon by the complainant in support of the complaint.

5.   Complaints can be submitted in any language in common use in the area of the Region where elections are being held, or in English.

6.   Once the UNTAES Election Field Office and the LEC receive a complaint they will either

a)   Attempt to resolve the complaint informally within 48 hours or

b)   Immediately refer the complaint to the UNTAES Electoral Unit in Vukovar if the complaint relates to either a violation of Croatian legislation or a serious violation of rules and procedures established by the JIC.

7.   No anonymous complaints will be accepted.

8.   All complaints shall be public.

Section 3

Disposition of Complaints

1.   Every complaint, upon receipt by the UNTAES Electoral Unit, will be immediately reviewed to ensure compliance with the provisions of Sect ion 2. In the event that the complaint does not meet the requirements of Section 2, the complainant will be notified and will be required to supply such additional information as will fulfil the requirement of Section 2. Every complaint meeting the requirements of Section 2 will be assigned a file number.

2.   Once a complaint is filed, the UNTAES Electoral Unit will, if appropriate, have 48 hours to have the complaint adjudicated by the EAC.

Section 4

Election Appeals Commission

1.   The EAC is established and appointed by the JIC as an independent body to adjudicate electoral complaints. It submits opinions and recommendations to the TA, who has final authority, to resolve all electoral complaints.

2.   The EAC shall be composed of five members appointed by the Chair of the JIC in consultation with its members:

a)   Two senior judges or other lawyers from Croatia;

b)   Two senior judges or other lawyers from the local Serb community;

c)   One international judge or other lawyer with election experience who will serve as the Chair. The Chair will decide on all procedural matters.

3.   The EAC will fix its seat in Vukovar. The Chair may order the sitting of the EAC other than at its official seat, if he or she deems it necessary to facilitate the operation

of its proceedings. In such cases, the EAC will sit in the place where the facts under adjudication occurred.

4. The EAC will be served by the UNTAES Electoral Unit. UNTAES will provide legal counsel from among its staff to investigate and prepare draft opinions on complaints for consideration by the EAC.

5. The EAC will remain active until all complaints are adjudicated and will thereupon be disbanded by the JIC. Not later than five days after election day, the Chair of the EAC will submit a final report to the JIC and to the TA outlining the types of problems raised in the complaints, how they were adjudicated by the EAC and an overall assessment of their impact on free and fair elections.

Section 5

Jurisdiction of the Election Appeals Commission

1. The EAC will adjudicate complaints regarding:

a) Violations of Croatian electoral legislation, including, but not limited to: The Law on the Election of Members of Representative Bodies of Local Self-Government and Local Administration and Self-Government Units;

b) Serious violations of the present Code of Conduct;

c) Serious violations of other rules or procedures established by the JIC.

2. The EAC may issue advisory opinions to the TA, through the JIC, or institute proceedings for the purpose of assisting the electoral process.

3. The EAC shall apply to the JIC if it determines that situations have arisen which require modifications of the rules and procedures established by the JIC.

4. The EAC will endeavour to adjudicate any complaint within 48 hours from their filing by the UNTAES Electoral Unit.

5. The EAC may recommend the dismissal of a complaint at ant time after it has been submitted where the complaint is determined to be without merit or beyond the jurisdiction of the EAC.

6. In order to adjudicate complaints, the EAC will sit with the attendance of at least the Chair and two of its members. The attendance of all of the members of the EAC will be required to decide on matter of special importance, according to the decision of the Chair.

7. The EAC may call witnesses, consult with local authorities and solicit all evidence it deems appropriate.

8. The EAC will provide written opinions on all complaints adjudicated. These opinions will contain recommendations to the TA, through the JIC, on appropriate action to be taken.

9. Opinions of the EAC will be public while its deliberations are private and shall remain secret.

10. Any opinion reached on a complaint shall be based on the consensus of the members participating. If a consensus cannot be reached and this results in a tie, the Chair will break the tie.

Section 6

Opinions and Recommendations

1.   In issuing its opinions, the EAC will take the following into account:

a)   Responsibility of party leaders for their actions and those of party members;

b)   Responsibility of candidates on party lists for their actions and those of their sympathizers;

c)   Responsibility of independent candidates for their actions and those of their sympathizers;

d)   Responsibility of election officials for their actions.

2.   All opinions will contain recommendations on appropriate action to be taken on the complaint. Depending on the facts of the case under consideration, the EAC may recommend:

a)   Action to be taken to rectify acts which have resulted in violations of Croatian electoral legislation, the present Code and other rules and procedures established by the JIC. Such action may include ceasing an act or, in the case of any omission, performing any act specified;

b)   Action to be taken against any person, registered political party, election official or association which has committed a violation of Croatian electoral legislation, the present Code and the rules and procedures established by the JIC, including the removal of an election official from his or her post.

c)   The annulment of the result of an election in a particular electoral unit and the scheduling of a date for another election.

3.   The authority to make a final determination on all complaints regarding electoral violations rests with the TA. After considering any recommendation made by the EAC, the TA shall take whatever action he deems necessary.

Final Provisions

1.   In the event of a discrepancy between the English and Croatian versions of this Code, the English version will prevail.

2.   This Code of Conduct shall come into effect upon the formal announcement by the TA of the election date for the Region of Eastern Slavonia, Baranja and Western Sirmium.

Issued in Vukovar, Republic of Croatia, on 5 March 1977

JACQUES PAUL KLEIN, Transitional Administrator
for Eastern Slavonia, Baranja and Western Sirmium

ANNEX 2:

LIBERIA: SPECIAL ELECTIONS CODE OF CONDUCT 1997

1.   The Independent Elections Commission (IECOM), has determined that all officially registered political parties, their leaders, members and supporters, shall abide by this Election Code of Conduct, in the interest of free and fair elections during the 1997 Special Elections in Liberia.

2.   The fundamental right of a free and fair election, including the freedom to campaign nationwide, is the prerogative of all officially recognized political parties and persons which they are entitled to, and shall hereby enjoy, by virtue of this code of conduct.

3.   The right and freedom of each and all political parties to campaign and disseminate their political messages, principles and manifestos without let, fear or hindrance, shall be respected by all rival political parties, and to that end, all contesting parties and their candidates shall obey the following rules:

(a)   Intimidation and coercion

All officially registered and recognized political parties are free to function without fear of intimidation or coercion by rival political parties or other vested interests. Accordingly, acts of intimidation or coercion, in whatever form, are hereby prohibited and all participating political parties shall take appropriate steps to emphasize and reinforce the prohibition of such acts.

(b)   Weapons ban

The existing ban on carrying weapons of any kind is hereby reiterated and shall be strictly enforced. Accordingly, the possession and use of any kind of weapon, or of any instrument capable of being used as a weapon, shall be a sanctionable offence, particularly at any political rally, meeting, march or demonstration. Party/Coalition leaders are to sensitize members to this prohibition by having it printed and disseminated in their Party/Coalition manuals, instructions and orders.

(c)   Political rallies and meetings

All parties shall avoid any coincidences, in time or place, of their rallies, meetings and marches without those of other parties. All parties shall, therefore, be required to file with the Commission, and also cause to be published at least 72 hours in advance, details of their public rallies or marches in any particular district or locality. They shall also be expected to liaise and co-operate with the relevant Electoral District Magistrate and shall comply with all orders aimed at avoiding a clash or confrontation.

All Parties, their members and supporters shall refrain from interfering with or disrupting the meetings, rallies and marches of other parties and to that end, shall in good faith endeavour at all times to respect in speeches, broadcasts, press statements, posters, etc., the use of offensive or inflammatory language calculated to cause offence or incite to violence.

(d)   Equal and fair access

All political parties, and particularly the leadership, shall scrupulously ensure freedom and equality of access of other parties to all potential voters on public property, in camps or reception centres or wherever such concentration of voters are located. They shall also adhere to guidelines designed to regulate and control access by all parties to all existing public communications facilities.

All political parties should enjoy equal and fair access to radio and all other mass communication media, in order to guarantee a 'level playing field' to all election candidates. Accordingly, the Independent Elections Commission shall establish firm guidelines to regulate and control access by the parties to all existing public communications facilities.

All Parties shall designate their representatives to attend at least once every week, briefing meetings under the Chairmanship of the Commission to discuss any matters of concern relating to voters registration or campaign. In addition, Party/Coalition leaders shall attend a weekly meeting presided over by the Chairman of the Independent Elections Commission. Emergency meetings can also be held at the instance of the Chairman of the Commission, if such a need arises.

All Parties are expected to behave with responsibility. To this end, parties shall not abuse the right to complain or knowingly and maliciously make false, frivolous or vexations complaints against their rivals.

(e)   Secret ballots

All political parties shall consistently emphasize and reinforce to their supporters and to all voters that balloting will be in secret, so that there is no fear of victimization. In addition, parties shall constantly remind their supporters of the need to observe the Elections Law, this Code of Conduct and all other rules promulgated by the Commission in connection with the conduct of these elections. Parties must, obligatorily, educate their supporters that tampering with ballots cast either by rigging or falsification of any kind is a criminal offence carrying serious and enforceable legal sanctions, whether in the capacity of a perpetrator, an accessory after the fact, accomplice or facilitator.

(f)   Exerting undue influence

Political parties shall not, whatever the temptation, procure votes by forcible occupation of polling stations or through other illegal activities at the polling stations.

Parties shall not attempt to influence the outcome of the balloting through monetary inducement in the form of bribery or allurement of election officials. Everyone, including both the giver and the receiver, should be aware that is a serious electoral offence with enforceable sanctions.

ANNEX 3:

PAKISTAN: CODE OF CONDUCT FOR THE POLITICAL PARTIES AND CONTESTING CANDIDATES: GENERAL ELECTIONS 1997

Election Commission of Pakistan
Notification
Islamabad, the 17th December 1996

S.R.O. 1376(1)/96. In pursuance of the provisions of Article 218(3) of the Constitution of the Islamic Republic of Pakistan, the Election Commission is pleased to lay down the following Code of Conduct for the Political Parties and the Contesting Candidates for General Elections, 1997:-

Code of Conduct for the Political Parties
And Contesting Candidates for General
Elections, 1997

(1)   The political parties shall not propagate any opinion, or act in any manner prejudicial to the ideology of Pakistan, or the sovereignty, integrity or security of Pakistan, or morality, or the maintenance of public order, or the integrity or independence of the judiciary of Pakistan, or which defames or brings into ridicule the judiciary or the armed forces of Pakistan, as provided under Article 63 of the Constitution.

(2)   The political parties, their candidates, agents or workers shall not obstruct or break up meetings organized by the rival parties and candidates, nor interrupt speeches or prevent distribution of handbills and leaflets.

(3)   No person or political party shall affix hoarding, posters or banners of any size or cause wall chalking as a part of election campaign of a candidate. [Section 83A of the Representation of the People Act, 1976].

(4)   No person or a political party or a contesting candidate shall hoist or fix party flags on any public property or at any public place. [Section 83A of the Representation of the People Act, 1976].

(5)   There shall be ban on hoisting party flags on house roofs. Party flags shall be allowed to be displayed on party and election offices of political party.

(6)   No election camp shall be set up on any road or place meant for the use of the public. Election camp shall as far as possible be simple. No food or drink shall be served to the voters in the election camp.

(7)   No contesting candidate shall use more than three microphones in his constituency and the use of mikes shall be restricted between 11 am and 4 pm particularly in view of Ramazan-ul-Mubarik and Taraveeh Prayers. Loudspeakers shall not be used for election campaign except at the election meetings. [Section 83A of the Representation of the People Act, 1976.]

(8)   The processions of buses, trucks or any other vehicles or torch procession shall not be brought out by any political party or any contesting candidate in favour of a candidate.

(9)   Only the polling personnel, contesting candidates, election agent, polling agents and voters, shall have a right to enter the polling station. Workers of the political parties or candidates shall not enter the polling station. The polling agents, sitting on their allotted places, shall perform their specific duties.

(10) Parties and politicians should refrain from making references to secret and confidential matters, which were within their official knowledge when they were in power, nor should they betray the confidence which they enjoyed by virtue of their official position.

(11) Political parties and contesting candidates should discourage their workers from exerting undue pressure against the news media, including newspapers offices and presses or resort to violence of any kind against the media.

(12) Political parties and contesting candidates should refrain from making such comments on international issues as are likely to embarrass the government's relations with other countries, nor should they say any thing or do any act in any manner which might prejudice Pakistan's foreign relations. Controversial and harsh remarks about leaders of other countries and their ideologies should be avoided.

(13) Political parties should carry out a comprehensive plan for education of voters in the manner of marking the ballot paper and casting votes.

(14) The political parties shall avoid criticism of other political parties, their leaders and candidates having no bearing on their public activities. Criticism and comments shall be confined to policies and programmes of other parties. Speeches and slogans shall be dignified and based on principle of morality, decorum and decency.

(15) The political parties, contesting candidates and workers shall refrain from deliberate dissemination of false and malicious information and their workers shall not indulge in forgeries and disinformation to defame other political parties and their leaders, and use of abusive language against the leaders and candidates of their political parties.

(16) No leader or candidate of a political party shall call the leader or candidate of another party kafir or traitor.

(17) The political parties shall refrain from speeches calculated to arouse parochial and sectarian feelings and controversy or conflicts between genders, sects, communities and linguistic groups. (Section 78 of the Representation of the People Act, 1976].

(18) The political parties, contesting candidates and their workers shall not propagate against the participation of any person in the elections on the basis of sex.

(19) Public leaders and all other participants in political activity shall act with a sense of responsibility and dignity befitting their status. While propagating their own views and programmes, they shall not interfere with the freedom of others to do the same as that would be the negation of democracy.

(20) The political parties and contesting candidates shall not hold public meetings or rallies on main streets, roads and chowks to avoid traffic jams and public inconvenience.

(21) Appeals to violence or resort to violence during meetings, processions, or during polling hours shall be strictly avoided. [Section 81 of the Representation of People Act, 1976].

(22) No person shall in any manner cause injury to any person or damage to any property. (Section 81 of the Representation of the People Act, 1976].

(23) Carriage of lethal weapons and fire arms shall not be allowed in public meetings and processions and official regulations in this regard shall be strictly observed. Use of crackers and other explosives at public meetings shall not be allowed.

(24) The political parties and their candidates shall extend cooperation to the officers on election duty in order to ensure peaceful and orderly polling and complete freedom for the voters to exercise their franchise without being subjected to any annoyance or obstructions. [Section 86 of the Representation of the People Act, 1976].

(25) The political parties and their candidates shall scrupulously avoid all activities which are 'corrupt practices' and offences under the election law, such as the bribing of voters, intimidation of voters, impersonation of voters, canvassing within 400 yards of a polling station, holding public meetings during the period of 48 hours ending with the hour fixed for the close of the poll. [Sections 78, 84 and 85 of the Representation of the People Act, 1976].

(26) The political parties, contesting candidates, agents or workers shall not indulge in offering gifts or gratifications or inducing another to stand or not to stand as a candidate, or to withdraw or not to withdraw his candidature. [Section 79 of the Representation of the People Act, 1976].

(27) No contesting candidate or a political party shall, under any circumstances, cross the limit of election expenses—rupees one million for the National Assembly and rupees six hundred thousands for the Provincial Assembly seats. [Section 49 of the Representation of the People Act, 1976].

(28) A political party may, at the national level, publish or broadcast or cause to be published or broadcast advertisements as a part of its election campaign; total expenses of such publication, broadcast or advertisement shall not exceed thirty million rupees. [Section 83B of the Representation of People Act, 1976].

(29) Concerned political parties and contesting candidates may announce their overall development programme. But following the announcement of the election schedule till the day of polling, no candidate or any person on his behalf shall, openly or in secret, give any subscription or donation, or make promise for giving such subscription or donation, to any institution of their respective constituency or to any other institution, nor shall commit to undertake any development project in the respective constituency.

(30) Ministers shall not combine their official visits with electioneering work.

(31) The local police administration and the opposite party shall, in advance, be informed of the date, time and place for holding meetings or processions in favour of any contending political party or candidate. The organizers of any meeting shall have to seek the assistance of the police for taking action against the persons who obstruct to the holding of such meeting or create disturbances in such meeting. The organizers shall not themselves take any action against such persons.

(32) The political parties and contesting candidates should not procure the support or assistance of any civil servant to promote or hinder the election of a candidate. [Section 83 of the Representation of the People Act, 1976].

(33) The political parties and their candidates shall dissuade their workers or sympathizers from destroying any ballot paper or any official mark on the ballot paper. [Section 87 of the Representation of the People Act, 1976].

By order of the Election Commission of Pakistan.

Sgd.

Khan Ahmed Goraya

Secretary

ANNEX 4:

BANGLADESH: CODE OF CONDUCT FOR ELECTIONS 1996

Ban on Donation or Subscription

The political parties may announce their overall development planning. But from the date of announcement of the election schedule until the polling is completed, the contending parties and candidates may not donate or commit to donate any sum of money, publicly or secretly, to any institution of their respective constituencies. During that period they may not commit to adopt any development project in their respective areas.

Use of Dak Bungalows and Rest Houses

All parties and candidates will enjoy equal rights in using government rest houses, circuit houses or dak bungalows on the basis of their application and in accordance with the existing principles in this regard. But officials engaged in election duties will get priority in using the facilities of rest houses, circuit houses or dak bungalows.

Election Campaign

(1)   All political parties and candidates will enjoy equal rights with regard to election campaigns. Rallies, processions or other election campaigns of the opponents can not be disrupted or obstructed.

(2)   The contending parties and candidates must inform the police authorities and their opponents of the date, time and venue of their respective rallies or marches ahead of time.

(3)   The contending parties and candidates must inform the police of the time and venue of their rallies in advance so that the authorities may take necessary measures for public movement and ensure law and order.

(4)   No public meeting may be held on any road disrupting the movement of people without the permission of appropriate authorities.

(5)   Organisers of any rally, meeting or other programme must report to the police if their programme is disturbed by trouble makers. The organisers must not take measures against the trouble-makers on their own.

(6)   Following the announcement of the polling schedule, no political party or candidate may use government media, official transportation, government officials or employees or other state facilities.

(7)   No posters, leaflets, or handbills may be put on the posters, leaflets of handbills of the rival candidates.

(8)   No election camps may be set up on the roads or places of public use. Election camps should be simple, as far as possible; voters cannot be entertained with any sort of food or drinks in the election camps.

(9)   Government dak bungalows, rest houses, circuit houses or any government office cannot be used as a place for election campaign.

(10) Posters for election campaigns must be printed on country-made paper in black and white and cannot be more than 22″ × 18″ in size.

(11) No contender should use more than three microphones at a time in his respective area and the use of mikes will be limited between 2 pm and 8 pm.

(12) Lands, buildings or other movable or immovable property of any citizen must not be damaged in connection with the election and personal peace of any person must not be violated by undesired activities or undisciplined behaviour.

(13) All contenders will refrain from all sorts of wall writings as a means of election campaign.

(14) In the interest of maintaining law and order, no motor vehicles, including motor cycles, can be moved and no sort of firearms or explosives can be carried within the premises of polling centres; no government official or local influential persons can illegally intervene in election activities.

(15) Truck or bus or torch processions on behalf of any candidate are banned.

(16) All political parties and candidates must cooperate with the officials and employees engaged in election duties to ensure completion of voting in a disciplined manner without any trouble.

(17) No political party or candidate can give any unpalatable or provocative statement and say anything which might hurt the sentiment of the followers of any religion.

(18) No contender will in any way exceed the fixed limit of the election expenditure.

Keeping the Election Free of any Influence

The election must not be influenced by money, weapons, muscle power or local influence.

Access to the Polling Centre

Only the employees and officials engaged in election duties, rival candidates, polling agents and voters will have access to the polling centres. No worker of any political party or candidate will be allowed freedom of movement inside the polling centres. Only the polling agents, sitting in their fixed places, may perform their specific duties.

Pre-Polling Irregularities

Violation of any clause of the code will be considered as pre-polling irregularities and any person or political party aggrieved by such violation can apply to the electoral inquiry committee or the Election Commission to seek remedy. If the application filed to the Election Commission is found to be objective, the commission may send it to the concerned or any electoral inquiry committee for investigation. In both the cases the electoral inquiry committee after investigation under Article 91A of the Representation of People Order 1972 (P. O. No 155 of 1972) will submit a recommendation to the Commission.

ANNEX 5:

BOSNIA AND HERZEGOVINA

Organization for Security and Cooperation in Europe
Rules and Regulations of the Provisional Election Commission
VII Codes

Electoral Code of Conduct for Political Parties, Candidates and Election Workers

Article 119

The object of this Code is to promote conditions conducive to the conduct of a free and fair election and a climate of democratic tolerance in which political activity can take place during the election period without fear of coercion, intimidation or reprisals. The Code is binding on all political parties and candidates, who must declare their acceptance of it before being registered by the Provisional Election Commission. It is the responsibility of political parties and candidates to ensure that the Code is strictly observed by all their representatives, campaign workers and active supporters.

Article 120

The following actions are strictly forbidden by the Provisional Election Commission:

(1)   The carrying or display of arms or weapons at political meetings, polling stations, or in the course of any gathering of a political party nature.

(2)   The use on polling day of any communications device in a polling station, or any loudspeaker or public address system whether mobile or fixed within hearing distance of a polling station;

(3)   The exhibiting of any form of propaganda, campaign material or advertisement on or in a polling station;

(4)   OSCE Supervisors with the help of local police forces and, where appropriate, of the International Police Task Force will ensure that these prohibitions are observed.

Article 121

All registered political parties and candidates must commit themselves to acknowledge the authority of the Provisional Election Commission; to implement and abide by its Rules and Regulations; to facilitate the access of its Members, official Supervisors and monitors, and other representatives, including accredited members of the OSCE Mission, to all public political meetings and other electoral activities; and to take all possible steps to ensure their safety from exposure to insult, hazard or threat in the course of their official duties.

Article 122

All registered parties and candidates will respect the right of other parties and candidates participating in the elections to conduct their campaigns in a peaceful environment, to hold public meetings and to have access to all forms of public media in order to explain their policies, to canvass freely for membership and support from the voters, and to publish and distribute notices of meetings, placards, posters and other written publicity material. They will refrain from disruption of meetings held by other parties and candidates and will not use, or incite others to use, any form of violence or intimidation against other parties and candidates or their supporters. They will respect the freedom of the press and will refrain from any harassment or obstruction of journalists in the pursuit of their professional activities. They will refrain from offering any inducement or reward to voters in return for their support, and from any threat of retaliation or reprisal against supporters of other parties and candidates.

Article 123

Any party or individual who has reason to believe that a party or candidate in the election has committed a breach of this Code of Conduct will have the right to lodge a complaint with the appropriate Election Commission or directly with the Provisional Election Commission, which will have the power to impose appropriate penalties, ranging from fines to disqualification of individual candidates or of one or more of the candidates appearing on a party list.

Article 124

All political parties and candidates pledge themselves to accept the result of the elections once these have been certified by the Provisional Election Commission.

Regulations Concerning the Obligations of Governments in Relation to the Media in Bosnia and Herzegovina[255]

Article 125

The Governments will permit journalists to enjoy complete freedom of movement and unhindered pursuit of their professional activities throughout Bosnia and Herzegovina. Journalists who are citizens of Bosnia and Herzegovina shall exercise this right on the basis of an identification card issued by their media organization or by an appropriate professional association. Accreditation cards will be identical in both Entities, and will only state the name of the journalist, the specific media for which he or she works, and the date of expiration, and should include a photograph. Foreign journalists shall exercise their rights on the basis of accreditation already issued by the

---

[255] The Media Experts Commission will ensure that the media themselves observe the Standards of Professional Conduct.

appropriate authorities in Bosnia and Herzegovina or to be issued in the future by the Media Experts Commission and such accreditation will be valid in the entire territory of Bosnia and Herzegovina.

Article 126

The Governments recognize that the profession of journalism is an important service to the public, and will not impose any sanctions or penalties on journalists, nor subject them to detention, harassment or interference of any kind, in pursuit of their legitimate professional activities.

Article 127

The Governments, in accordance with the provisions of paragraph 7 of the Agreed Measures adopted in Geneva on 18 March 1996, will ensure that licenses and frequencies for electronic and print media are granted expeditiously, on the basis of objective non-political criteria, in order to ensure that all political parties and candidates in the elections have equitable access to the media.

Standards of Professional Conduct for the Media and Journalists[256]

Article 128

In the pursuance of their duties, members of the media as the servants of public interest must maintain the highest professional and ethical standards.

Article 129

Members of the media shall at all times defend the freedom of information and make a clear distinction between factual reporting and editorial comment.

Article 130

Members of the media shall ensure that the information they report is factually accurate, complete, fair, equitable and unbiased.

Article 131

Members of the media must avoid distortion, suppression, falsification, misrepresentation and censorship.

---

[256] The Provisional Election Commission has determined that compliance with the following Standards of Professional Conduct for the Media and Journalists will be essential for the conduct of free and fair elections in Bosnia and Herzegovina. These Standards are based upon the Constitution as set forth in Annex 4 of the General Framework Agreement for Peace in Bosnia and Herzegovina and particularly on Article II (3)(h). The Standards are derived from international agreements referred to in the Framework Section of the Peace Agreement, and Point 8 of the Appendix to Annex 6, as well as the 1990 Copenhagen Document of the OSCE Conference on the Human Dimension, attached to Annex 3.

Article 132

Members of the media must not abuse their professional rights by accepting bribes or any other inducement that might influence the exercise of their professional responsibilities.

Article 133

Members of the media ought to avoid language which encourages discrimination, ridicule, prejudice or hatred.

Article 134

Members of the media shall rectify, promptly and with due prominence, any inaccuracies, ensure appropriate correction and apologies and afford a right of reply.

Article 135

Members of the media shall protect their sources of information.

Article 136

Media are encouraged to develop and periodically review their editorial policies.

Media Experts Commission
(Extracts)

Article 145

A Media Experts Commission has been established in order to assist the Governments of the Parties to Annex 3 of the General Framework Agreement for Peace in Bosnia and Herzegovina in the fulfilment of their obligations in relation to the media, in particular with respect to freedom of movement, full and equal access of the media and all other media activities related to the elections. The Media Experts Commission will also ensure that the media themselves observe the Standards of Professional Conduct.

Article 149

The Commission and Sub-Commissions will have the responsibilities:

(a) to issue accreditation to foreign journalists and to act as the final arbiter in disputes concerning the accreditation of foreign journalists;

(b) to investigate allegations of falsification of journalists' accreditation cards, mistreatment of journalists and other media-related complaints, and to take or recommend to the Provisional Election Commission appropriate action;

(c) to monitor the fulfilment by the Parties of their obligations to ensure the security of journalists and their freedom of movement and unhindered pursuit of their professional activities; and, as necessary, make recommendations to the Provisional Election Commission;

(d) to monitor the performance of the media in providing equitable access for all political parties and candidates participating in the election campaign, and as necessary to take appropriate steps or make recommendations to the Provisional Election Commission;

(e) to arrange for monitoring of the media; to consider cases or complaints of erroneous news reporting or the use of inflammatory language by the media; to issue judgments on such complaints and insist on their full and prominent publication by the media concerned; and if necessary to refer them to the Provisional Election Commission.

Rules And Regulations For International Election Observers

Article 151

The Provisional Election Commission will invite International Observers in accordance with the General Framework Agreement for Peace in Bosnia and Herzegovina, Annex 3, Art III (e) and the Copenhagen Document, paragraph 8, which is an integrated component of the Dayton Peace Agreement. These Observers include representatives of governments and international organizations and representatives of international non-governmental organizations.

Article 152

The Provisional Election Commission will authorize the Election Monitoring Group to accredit the International Observers.

Article 153

International Observers will observe the electoral process in accordance with the Rules and Regulations of the Provisional Election Commission and they will not interfere in any way in electoral proceedings.

Article 154

The International Observers shall abide by the laws of Bosnia and Herzegovina and of the two entities and by the Code of Conduct for International Observers.

Article 155

International Observers shall be strictly impartial and politically neutral.

Article 156

The Coordinator of the Election Monitoring Group and his office will co-ordinate a joint effort of the International Observers to observe all aspects of the electoral process. International Observers will be present at polling stations and counting centres and their observations will be the basis of the overall assessment of the electoral process.

Article 157

The Coordinator of the Election Monitoring Group may report periodically and independently on the elections inside and outside the country. After the official announcement of the results the Coordinator of the Election Monitoring Group will make a final evaluation on the conduct of the election in a report to the Chairman in Office of the OSCE.

Article 158

The Election Monitoring Group shall be responsible for coordinating the operations and the security measures for the international observation.

Article 159

The International Observers shall have access to all relevant documents and meetings, shall be free to contact any person at any time during the entire period of the electoral process and shall have access to all polling stations and counting centres.

ANNEX 6:

INDIA: MODEL CODE OF CONDUCT FOR THE GUIDANCE OF POLITICAL PARTIES AND CANDIDATES 1996

Election Commission of India

I.   General Conduct

1.   No party or candidate shall indulge in any activity which may aggravate existing differences or create mutual hatred or cause tension between different castes and communities, religious or linguistic.

2.   Criticism of other political parties, when made, shall be confined to their policies and programme, past record and work. Parties and candidates shall refrain from criticism of all aspects of private life, not connected with the public activities of the leaders or workers of other parties. Criticism of other parties or their workers based on unverified allegations or on distortion shall be avoided.

3.   There shall be no appeal to caste or communal feelings for securing votes. Mosques, Churches, Temples or other places of worship shall not be used as forum for election propaganda.

4.   All parties and candidates shall avoid scrupulously all activities which are 'corrupt practices' and offences under the election law, such as the bribing of voters, intimidation of voters, personation of voters, canvassing within 100 meters of a polling station, holding public meetings during the period of 48 hours ending with the hours fixed for the close of the poll, and the transport and conveyance of voters to and from polling station.

5.   The right of every individual for peaceful and undisturbed home life shall be respected, however much the political parties or candidates may resent his/her political opinions or activities. Organising demonstration or picketing before the houses of individuals by way of protesting against their opinions or activities shall not be resorted to under any circumstances.

6.   No political party or candidate shall permit its or his/her followers to make use of any individual's land, building, compound wall etc., without his permission for erecting flag staffs, suspending banners, pasting notices, writing slogans, etc.

7.   Political parties and candidates shall ensure that their supporters do not create obstructions in or break up meetings and processions organised by the other parties. Workers or sympathizers of one political party shall not create disturbances at public meetings organized by another political party by putting question orally or in writing or by distributing leaflets of their own party. Processions shall not be taken out by one party along places at which meetings are being held by another party. Posters issued by one party shall not be removed by workers of another party.

II.   Meetings

1.   The party or candidate shall inform the local police authorities of the venue and time of any proposed meetings well in time so as to enable the police to make necessary arrangements for controlling traffic and maintaining peace and order.

2.   A party or candidate shall ascertain in advance if there are any restrictive or prohibitory orders in force in the place proposed for the meetings. If such orders exist, they shall be followed strictly. If any exemption is required from such orders it shall be applied for and obtained well in time.

3.   If permission or license is to be obtained for the use of loudspeakers or any other facility in connection with any proposed meeting, the party or candidate shall apply to the authority concerned well in advance and obtain such permission or license.

4.   Organisers of a meeting shall invariably seek the assistance of the police on duty for dealing with persons disturbing a meeting or otherwise attempting to create disorder. Organisers themselves shall not take action against such persons.

III.   Processions

1.   A party or candidate organising a procession shall decide before hand the time and place of the starting of the procession, the route to be followed and the time and place at which the procession will terminate. There shall ordinarily be no deviation from the programme.

2.   The organisers shall give advance intimation to the local police authorities of the programme so as to enable the latter to make necessary arrangements.

3.   The organisers shall ascertain if any restrictive orders are in force in the localities through which the procession has to pass, and shall comply with the restrictions unless exempted specially by competent authority. Any traffic regulations or restrictions shall also be carefully adhered to.

4.   The organisers shall take steps in advance to arrange for passage of the procession so that there is no block or hindrance to traffic. If the procession is very long, it shall be organised in segments of suitable lengths so that at convenient intervals, especially at points where the procession has to pass road junctions, the passage of held-up traffic could be allowed by stages, thus avoiding heavy traffic congestion.

5.   Processions shall be so regulated as to keep as much to the right of the road as possible and the direction and advice of the police on duty shall be strictly complied with.

6.   If two or more political parties or candidates propose to take processions over the same route or parts thereof at about the same time, the organisers shall establish contact well in advance and decide upon the measures to be taken to see that the processions do not clash or cause hindrance to traffic. The assistance of the local police shall be availed of for arriving at a satisfactory arrangement. For this purpose the parties shall contact the police at the earliest opportunity.

7.   The political parties or candidates shall exercise control to the maximum extent possible in the matter of processionists carrying articles which may be put to misuse by undesirable elements, especially in moments of excitement.

8.   The carrying of effigies purporting to represent members of other political parties or their leaders, burning such effigies in public and such other forms of demonstration shall not be countenanced by any political party or candidate.

IV. Polling Day

All political parties and candidates shall:

(i)   co-operate with the officers on election duty to ensure peaceful and orderly polling and complete freedom to the voters to exercise their franchise without being subjected to any annoyance or obstruction;

(ii)   supply to their authorised workers suitable badges or identity cards;

(iii) agree that the identity slips supplied by them to voters shall be plain (white) papers and shall not contain any symbol, name of the candidate or the name of the party;

(iv)   refrain from serving or distributing liquor on polling day and during twenty-four hours preceding it;

(v)   not allow unnecessary crowds to be collected near the camps set up by the political parties and candidates near the polling booths so as to avoid confrontation and tension among workers and sympathizers of the parties and candidates;

(vi)   ensure that the candidate's camps shall be simple. They shall not display any posters, flags, symbols or any other propaganda material. No eatables shall be served or crowds allowed at the camps; and

(vii) co-operate with the authorities in complying with the restrictions to be imposed on the plying of vehicles on the polling day and obtain permits for them which should be displayed prominently on those vehicles.

V. Polling Booth

Excepting the voters, no one without a valid pass from the Election Commission shall enter the polling booths.

VI. Observers

The Election Commission is appointing observers. If the candidates or their agents have any specific complaint or problem regarding the conduct of the elections they may bring the same to the notice of the observer.

VII. Party in Power

The party in power, whether at the centre or in the State or States concerned, shall ensure that no cause is given for any complaint that it has used its official position for the purposes of its election campaign, and in particular:

(i)(a) The Ministers shall not combine their official visit with electioneering work and shall also not make use of official machinery or personnel during electioneering work;

 (b)   Government transport including official aircrafts, vehicles, machinery and personnel shall not be used for furtherance of the interest of the party in power;

(ii)   Public places such as maidans etc., for holding election meetings, and use of helipads for airflights in connection with elections, shall not be monopolised by itself. Other parties and candidates shall be allowed the use of such places and facilities on the same terms and conditions on which they are used by the party in power;

(iii)   Rest houses, dak bungalows or other Government accommodation shall not be monopolised by the party in power or its candidates and such accommodation shall be allowed to be used by other parties and candidates in a fair manner but no party or candidate shall use or be allowed to use such accommodation (including premises appertaining thereto) as a campaign office for holding any public meeting for the purposes of election propaganda;

(iv)   Issue of advertisement at the cost of public exchequer in the newspapers and other media and the misuse of official mass media during the election period for partisan coverage of political news and publicity regarding achievements with a view to furthering the prospects of the party in power shall be scrupulously avoided.

(v)   Ministers and other authorities shall not sanction grants/payments out of discretionary funds from the time elections are announced by the Commission;

(vi)   From the time the elections are announced by the Commission, Ministers and other authorities shall not:-

   (a) Announce any financial grants in any form or promises thereof; or

   (b) Lay foundation stones etc., of projects or schemes of any kind; or

   (c) Make any promise of construction of roads, provision of drinking water facilities, etc.; or

   (d) Make any ad hoc appointments in Government, public undertakings etc., which may have effect or influencing the voters in favour of the party in power.

(vii)   Ministers of Central or State Government shall not enter any polling station or place of counting except in their capacity as a candidate or voter or authorised agent.

Reissued 1996

T.N. Seshan
Chief Election Commissioner of India
New Delhi, January 1996

ANNEX 7:

ST KITTS AND NEVIS: CODE OF CONDUCT FOR THE POLITICAL PROCESS

Ethical Guidelines Issued by St. Kitts Christian Council, Nevis Christian Council, St. Kitts Evangelical Association, Nevis Evangelical Association
June 1995

General Elections Ethical Guidelines

Pursuant to the Code of Conduct for the Political Process which was issued in 1993, The St. Kitts Christian Council, the St. Kitts Evangelical Association, the Nevis Christian Council and the Nevis Evangelical Association now issue Guidelines for Elections in St. Kitts and Nevis.

In our democracy, different strategies for social and economic development will be presented by the various political parties, and it is the people's right to make a choice through the process of General Elections. It is therefore the responsibility of all political leaders to propose the best way forward for all, especially for the poor or oppressed or marginalised.

However, electioneering is potentially divisive, and in the heat of campaigning it may be forgotten that we are one people. The following guidelines are being proposed in the interest of mature campaigning and fair and free elections. We therefore call on all concerned to accept and adhere to them:

A.   To the Electoral Commission

- The Electoral Commission should continue to be transparent and impartial.
- Ensure that any person who is eligible to vote and does so apply is properly registered.
- Any person who is eligible and properly registered to vote should not be denied the right to vote.

B.   To Candidates for Election, their Associates and Supporters

- Candidates in any General Election need to justify their suitability by presenting proposals for the betterment of St. Kitts and Nevis, its people and land, and its interaction with the Caribbean region and the world.
- The emphasis must be on issues rather than personalities.
- No abusive attacks or innuendos may be directed to campaigners or their family members for reasons of their race, social origins and background, education, gender, religion, or any other reason.
- Candidates must seek to be truthful about the past and present socio-economic state of St. Kitts and Nevis.

- Candidates must avoid raising unfulfillable expectations and making unrealistic promises.

- Care must be taken not to incite sectional hostility or violence.

- To further demonstrate political maturity and foster unity among the people, Parties not forming the Government should appeal to the Nation via the media to respect and acknowledge the Government formed by due process of the Constitution of the Federation.

- Campaign slogans and the like, affixed to walls, poles etcetera, should be such as are easily removable when campaigning ends. Special care should be taken to avoid defacing historic sites.

- Electoral regulations should be observed and not circumvented.

- Every person entitled to vote must be able to do so freely. Victimization of persons, interference with employment rights, intimidation, and the enticement with favours are gravely wrong.

- Avoid language that is abusive, indecent of inflammatory.

- When the election results have been finalized, unsuccessful candidates should accept defeat in the true spirit of sportsmanship and successful candidates should celebrate victory gracefully and humbly.

C. To Voters

- It is the individual's fundamental right to vote. A voter should not abstain from voting without good reason.

- All persons eligible to register should seek at all times to be honest with the information they impart.

- Do not sell your vote. You thereby forfeit your freedom of choice and devalue your worth as a person.

- Exercise your responsibility for the well-being of St. Kitts and Nevis by voting for a candidate of ability and integrity. Integrity would include adherence to the ethical guidelines herein.

- Integrity, good character, and sound judgement as manifested in your behaviour as a Voter is important to the Political Process, and those whom you seek to elect.

- Vote after serious consideration of all candidates' policies.

- Each person has a right to his or her views and to support the candidate he or she prefers. Respect must be maintained for the opinion of others.

- Each voter has a responsibility to obey the law and to promote the maintenance of law and order throughout the Federation.

D. To the Media

- Report the campaigning honestly and impartially.

- Ensure that news stories are accurate.

- ▪ Avoid the temptation to sensational reporting.
- ▪ Independent Candidates and Political Parties should be given equal time on the National Broadcasting Service.

To Be Signed by Leaders of Parties

We the undersigned candidates, who in the forthcoming elections will be leading other candidates seeking seats in the National Assembly of St. Kitts and Nevis, approve of the ethical guidelines issued by the St. Kitts Christian Council, the St. Kitts Evangelical Association, the Nevis Christian Council and the Nevis Evangelical Association, and pledge that we will put unreservedly into effect the guidelines provided for candidates, their associates and supporters, and request those whom we lead to do so.

To Be Signed by Independent Candidates

I the undersigned candidate, who will be seeking a seat in the National Assembly of St. Kitts and Nevis, approve of the Ethical Guidelines issued by the St. Kitts Christian Council, the St. Kitts Evangelical Association, the Nevis Christian Council and the Nevis Evangelical Association and pledge that I will put unreservedly into effect the guidelines provided for candidates, their associates and supporters.

ANNEX 8:

UNITED REPUBLIC OF TANZANIA

**The National Electoral Commission
Guidelines for the Coverage of the General Elections of 1995 by
the Government Owned Media
Presidential and Parliamentary General Elections
for the United Republic**

1.   Introduction

The Constitution of the United Republic guarantees freedom of opinion and expression that is to say, the right to hold and express opinions freely and to seek, receive and impart information and ideas through any media, whether through printed materials, or radio or television broadcasts. The media wield can assert (sic) enormous impact on society and can therefore play an important role in educating, informing and motivating the public for the common good. However, they can only achieve these lofty objectives if they deliberately adopt and observe certain guidelines and professional ethics for their editorial policy and in their handling of the factual news.

2.   These Guidelines shall apply after necessary consultations with parties has been finalised and shall be applicable up to 28th October 1995.

Guidelines for Government Owned Media During Election Campaign

3.   General Guidelines

(a)   Events

Reports of factual happenings should be accurate and without bias. Editorials and commentaries on events should be clearly distinguished from plain reports of events.

(b)   Controversial Issues

Where a public issue is controversial fair representation of the opposing sides should be afforded. Requests by any person or group to present their case on controversial public issues should be considered on their individual merits and in the light of their contribution to the public interest.

4.   Specific Guidelines

(a)   Access by Political Parties

(i)(a) The government owned media in mainland Tanzania consists of Radio Tanzania Dar es Salaam (RTD) and two newspapers — 'The Daily News' and 'The Sunday News'.

(b)   The government owned media in Zanzibar consist of Television Zanzibar (TVZ) and Radio Zanzibar which will be available after consultation between National Electoral Commission and Zanzibar Electoral Commission.

(ii)   Access to the government owned media shall be given free of charge and on an equal basis to all political parties which qualify and wish to campaign in the Presidential and Parliamentary Elections for the United Republic. Accordingly broadcasts should devote an equal period of time and the print media should make available the same amount of space for each qualified political party. The National Electoral Commission shall notify the media of the parties that qualify for this free coverage. The existing programmes aired by RTD available for political campaigning are:-

   (a)   News Bulletins

   (b)   TUAMBIE

   (c)   MAJIRA.

These programmes should be apportioned fairly and equitably among the Presidential and Vice Presidential Candidates and the qualified political parties.

(iii) No paid political programme should be accepted by the government owned media for dissemination of such programme during the election campaign save for 'kipindi maalum' to be facilitated by the National Electoral Commission.

(iv)

   (a)   Submission of Programmes

Programmes should be submitted by a political party concerned within seven days before the expected allocated time or space for publication.

   (b)   Political Programmes submitted to the government owned media for publication shall be in accordance with allocated time or space. Any extra material shall be returned to the political party concerned.

   (c)   Controversial Materials

If any of the media believes that a political programme is not in good taste, or contrary to the public interest, security, peace or morality, they may reject the political message in question in the presence of the appointed representative of the political party concerned. However, specific details should be provided for the rejection and opportunity be given for changing the material to meet broadcast or publication standards.

   (d)   Correction of Errors by the Media

The media may not censor or alter in any manner any of the materials presented by the parties or candidates to rectify the broadcasting or publication of errors, except after the consultations with the party concerned.

(v)   Disclaimers

The media shall insert or publish a disclaimer whenever a political programme is published by their medium. The disclaimer shall be made by the same medium which made the publication.

(vi) Incumbency

It is the responsibility of publishers to ensure that they do not become the vehicles by which participants in the election unduly benefit from their incumbency in Government.

(B) Requirements

The Mass Media shall ensure that all the registered political parties will cooperate in abiding by the election guidelines during the campaign period.

National Electoral Commission
Coverage of the General Elections of 1995 by the Private News Media

Introduction

The Constitution of the United Republic guarantees freedom of opinion and expression that is to say, the right to hold and express opinions freely and to seek, receive and impart information and ideas through any media, whether through printed materials, or radio or television broadcasts. The media wield can assert enormous impact on society and can therefore play an important role in educating, informing and motivating the public for the common good. However, they can only achieve these lofty objectives if they deliberately adopt and observe certain guidelines and professional ethics for their editorial policy and in their handling of the factual news. It is common knowledge that election campaign period started on 30th August 1995 and will end on the 28th October, 1995.

Guidelines

In order to have before them the right kind of information on the candidates and party policies on which to base their choice, the voters will need a fair and unbiased coverage by the mass media.

The National Electoral Commission therefore urges the private media to observe the following points:

(a) News

To be fair and without bias in the reporting of factual happenings, which should be clearly distinguished from news analysis, commentaries and editorials. Professional ethics should be maintained in the use and selection of news sources.

(b) Controversial Public Issues

Opportunity for fair representation of opposing sides should be granted. Requests by individuals or groups to present their views on controversial public issues should be considered on the basis of merit and in the light of their bearing on the public interest.

(c)   Access by Political Parties to Gratuitous Programmes

The National Electoral Commission requests the broadcast media (radio and television) to make available, weekly and at no cost a reasonable amount of time or space, for each qualified political party to deliver political advertisements.

The National Electoral Commission shall notify the media of the political parties which qualify for this free coverage. All such programmes should be clearly identified as a public service to political parties.

(d)   Submission of Programmes

The media may establish reasonable deadlines for the submission of the materials in order to fit their broadcast or publication schedule.

The media shall ensure that all political parties are given equal treatment and access as to time and space for the publication of their political programmes.

(e)   Correction of Errors by the Media

The media may not censor or alter in any manner any of the materials presented by the parties or candidates to rectify the broadcasting or publication of errors, except after the consultations with the party concerned.

(f)   Controversial Materials

If any of the media believes that a political programme is not in good taste, or contrary to the public interest, security, peace or morality, they may reject the political message in question in the presence of the appointed representative of the political party concerned. However, specific details should be provided for the rejection and opportunity be given for changing the material to meet broadcast or publication standards.

(g)   Paid Political Advertisements

Political parties or candidates who require additional time and space should pay for all the extra advertisements, preferably at the lowest established rates, but each party should be charged at the same rate. However, one political party or candidate should not be allowed to block access by other parties or candidates by purchasing all available time or space.

ANNEX 9:

PALESTINE

Government of Israel – Palestine Liberation Organization, Declaration of Principles on Interim Self-Government Arrangements[257]

Annex II

Protocol concerning Elections

Article IV
The Election Campaign

1.   General campaign provisions

a.   All activities carried out by nominated candidates, or by political parties, coalitions, or groupings of electors who have nominated candidates, or for their benefit, that are directly addressed to obtain the electorate's vote, shall constitute campaign activities. Candidates and their supporter promote their campaign by any legal means.

b.   The official campaign period of the election, during which the provisions relating to the election campaign will apply, will start 22 days before polling day and close 24 hours before the polls open. Campaigning on the day before polling day, or on polling day itself, will not be permitted,

2.   Rallies and meetings

a.   The CEC will publish a list of venues and facilities available for election rallies and meetings, which shall include all recognized public open air meeting places and all public buildings with a recognized public meeting hall. The CEC will also publish a list of routes available for marches. These lists will be posted in each constituency in the respective DEO. Such campaign activities shall be conducted at venues and facilities included in the lists published by the CEC.

b.   Without derogating from the principle that the Palestinian Police will ensure public order during the Palestinian elections, and in order to enable the elections to proceed smoothly, without any interference, obstacle or friction, the two sides agree to deal with, and coordinate with regard to, security issues that may arise in relation to the electoral process in the relevant DCO in each constituency.

c.   Security issues relating to the international observers will also be dealt with in the relevant DCO, within the framework of the trilateral Palestinian-Israeli-European Union forum, as set out in Article V, paragraph 7 below.

---

[257]   32 *ILM* 1525 (1993).

d.   Each side shall take all necessary measures with regard to persons under its authority to prevent public disorder during campaign activities, to ensure that such activities do not interfere with the free flow of traffic, and to protect the electoral process from any violence, incitement, hostile propaganda or other undemocratic interference.

e.   (1) The representative of a candidate or candidates wanting to hold a rally, meeting or march must submit an application to the relevant DCO giving details of the proposed time and venue.

(2) With regard to applications to hold such a campaign activity in areas in which the Palestinian Police exercises responsibility order, but there is no Palestinian police station or post, the DEO shall give prior notification of the activity to the relevant DCO.

(3) With regard to applications to hold such a campaign activity outside the areas in which the Palestinian Police exercises responsibility for public order, the activity shall only take place after coordination and confirmation through the relevant DCO.

Article V
International Observation of Elections

1.   International Standards

The election process will be open to international observation. Observation will be conducted according to accepted international standards.

2.   Scope of observation

a.   All stages of the electoral process will be open to observation. This includes registration of electors, the campaign, the operation of polling stations during polling, the operation of the count in each polling station and the totalling and scrutiny (including the determination of claims made by candidates or their representatives) at district and central level.

b.   The observers will be asked to assess whether all stages of the electoral process are free and fair. The activity of the observers will be limited to observation, reporting and dialogue with the relevant authorities.

c.   Observer delegations may wish at any point to make comments or representations about the conduct of the elections to the CEC, which shall consider them and reply appropriately.

d.   In order to facilitate the independence of the observation, the mandate and operating instructions of each international observer delegation shall be determined by that delegation in consultation with the international observer coordinating body under the common terms of reference attached as Appendix 2 to this Annex.

3.   Source of observers

It is envisaged that observers will be present from all parts of the world.

a.   Observer delegation will, in particular be present from the European Union, the United Nations, the United States of America, the Russian Federation, Canada, Egypt, Japan, Jordan, Norway, South Africa, the Movement of Non-Aligned Nations, the Organization of African Unity and the Islamic Conference Organization. Observer delegations from other governments or inter-governmental organizations may be added to this list upon consultation.

b.   Other observers, including those representing non-governmental organizations, will also be present.

4.   Coordinating body

The European Union will act as the coordinator for the activity of observer delegations.

5.   Accreditation of observers

a.   All observers, both international and domestic, shall be accredited through machinery established by the CEC. Accreditation will be issued by the CEC on request and will be conditional on acceptance of the common terms of reference. The accreditation card will contain a trilingual text (Arabic, English and Hebrew).

b.   The accreditation card of members of observer delegations and member the Coordinating Body shall contain the following details:

    (1) full name;

    (2) country of origin;

    (3) the following text: 'The bearer of this card is an International Observer and is entitled to Privileges and Immunities in accordance with the Interim Agreement'; and

    (4) a photograph.

c.   The accreditation card of other observers shall not be the same colour as the card for members of observer delegations in subparagraph b. above, and shall contain the following details:

    (1) name;

    (2) organization;

    (3) the words 'Election Observer';

    (4) the following text: 'The bearer of this card is an Election Observer entitled to all possible assistance in the conduct of his or her tasks in accordance with the Interim Agreement'; and

    (5) a photograph.

6.   Privileges and immunities

a.   Observer delegations and members of the coordinating body (hereinafter 'delegation members') shall be granted, according to international standards, the privileges and immunities necessary for the fulfilment of their activities in accordance with Appendix 3 to this Annex.

b.   The names of delegation members will be supplied in advance by the CEC to Israel, following which privileges and immunities will be granted in accordance with Appendix 3.

7.   Trilateral coordination forum for logistics and security

The CEC, Israel and the European Union shall establish a trilateral forum for the purpose of dealing with issues (for example: security of observers, communications, visas, identification, and other questions of logistics) which are raised by observer delegations as requiring assistance, or which otherwise require coordination between the members of the trilateral forum. Other matters relating to the conduct of the elections may be dealt with between the CEC and the European Union bilaterally. The operational modalities of the trilateral forum will be agreed by the parties at its first meeting,

8.   Freedom of movement

a.   For the purposes of election observation, all measures necessary will be taken to ensure freedom of movement in all areas of operation.

b.   Observers will not be accompanied by official representatives of the CEC or of Israel unless they so request.

9.   Equipment of observers

a.   Members of observer delegations will be identifiable by a distinctive outfit (cap, shirt, jacket etc.) and an overjacket carrying the words 'International Observer' in Arabic and English. Other observers will be otherwise identified.

b.   Observers will not carry arms.

10.   Reporting by observer delegations

During and following the election, the coordinating body, each individual observer delegation, and other observers may issue statements and hold press conferences as to their findings.

11.   Domestic observers and parallel vote tabulations

Domestic observer organizations will be required to be independent of parties, coalitions and groupings of electors with nominated candidate(s) and will be accredited by the CEC on request. Domestic observer organizations will operate under the common terms of reference for domestic observers attached in Appendix 2. Any parallel vote tabulation organization will also be accredited as a domestic observer organization.

12.   Provisions for Journalists

Domestic and international journalists will be accredited by the CEC upon production of valid press documentation. Journalists shall enjoy freedom of the press and of movement in all areas in order to cover the electoral process. Journalists shall have access to all electoral facilities during all stages of the electoral process. The electoral authorities may request the presentation of the issued accreditation in order to facilitate this access.

Appendix 2

Common Terms of Reference for Observers

A.   International Observers

1.   Observers are invited to observe the full Palestinian election process, from the announcement through registration, campaign, polling, counting, compiling of results and complaints procedures.

2.   All bodies sending observers will be free in their choice of observers. All observers will be issued on arrival with accreditation by the CEC.

3.   Any accredited observer is free to have contact with any person at any time and anywhere and to attend all election related events.

4.   Israel will allow accredited observers to travel through and to get accommodation in Israel.

5.   The premises, equipment and property, including papers, documents (including computerized documents), communications, correspondence and databases of observer organizations shall be respected by each side according to its applicable laws. This provision shall apply also to the property of observers created, maintained or used for the purposes of their work or duties.

6.   Members of observer delegations will wear their distinctive outfit (caps, shirts, jackets, etc., including the words 'INTERNATIONAL OBSERVER' in Arabic

and English) whenever and wherever they go on duty. Observers who are not members of observer delegations in accordance with Article V, paragraph 3 of this Annex (hereinafter 'other observers') will be otherwise identified.

7.   All observers will be responsible for the arrangement of their own accommodation, equipment, means of transport, and medical and other insurance.

8.   The CEC and Israel will bear no financial liability in respect of expenditure undertaken by observers, or of injury, damage or loss incurred by observers in the course of their duties or otherwise. The European Union will only bear such liability in relation to members of the coordinating body and to the European Union observers and only to the extent that it explicitly agrees so to do.

9.   No restriction shall be placed on introducing foreign currency to fund the activities of observers nor on the repatriation of such funds to any country abroad nor on the free exchange of foreign currency through an authorized dealer in exchange at the market rate of exchange.

10. All necessary measures shall be taken to ensure the security of observers. Enhanced security will be provided as necessary on request.

11. All observers have the right to emergency medical assistance, including emergency evacuation as necessary. The appropriate Israeli authorities undertake to provide such emergency assistance and evacuation.

B.   Domestic Observers

1.   Domestic observers are invited to observe the full Palestinian election process, from the announcement through registration, campaign, polling, counting, compiling of results and complaints procedures.

2.   All domestic observer bodies will be free in their choice of observers. Domestic observers will be issued with accreditation by the CEC.

3.   Any accredited domestic observer is free to move and to have contact with any person at any time and anywhere and to attend all election related events.

4.   Freedom of speech for domestic observers in regard of words in their official capacity shall be guaranteed.

5.   The premises, equipment and property, including papers, documents (including computerized documents), communications, correspondence and databases of domestic observer organizations shall be respected by each side, according to its applicable laws. This provision shall apply also to the property of domestic observers created, maintained or used for the purposes of their work or duties.

6.   Israel will allow accredited domestic observers from the list provided by the CED to travel through Israel in the course of their duties.

7.   All observers will be responsible for the arrangement of their own equipment, means of transport, and medical and other insurance.

8.   The CEC and Israel will bear no financial liability in respect expenditure undertaken by observers, or of injury, damage or loss incurred by observers in the course of their duties or otherwise.

Appendix 3

Privileges and Immunities of International Observer Delegations

For the purpose of this Appendix, privileges and immunities shall be granted to all accredited members of international observer delegations, and members of the coordinating body and personnel appointed by observer delegations to perform activities related to the election observation (hereinafter 'delegation members').

1.   Delegation members shall:

    a.   be immune from personal arrest or detention, and from seizure of any personal belongings;

    b.   be immune from legal process in respect of words spoken or written or acts done by them in the course of the performance of their mission;

    c.   enjoy inviolability for all papers and documents, including computerized documentation; and

d.   be permitted, for the purposes of their official communications, to use codes and to receive papers and correspondence by courier or sealed bags.

2.   The inviolability and freedom of communications and correspondence to and from delegation members shall be assured.

3.   The premises, including all archives and databases, property, funds and assets of delegation members shall:

a.   be protected and inviolable; and

b.   be immune from search, requisition, confiscation, expropriation and any other form of interference, whether by executive, administrative, judicial or legislative action.

4.   Without prejudice to their privileges and immunities, it is the duty of all persons enjoying these privileges and immunities to respect the laws and regulations in force in the areas under each side's jurisdiction.

5.   The coordinating body and each observer delegation will be able to acquire and use freely and efficiently, from the beginning to the end of its operation, the means of communication necessary for it to fulfill its duty. Within the framework of the trilateral forum as defined in Article V, paragraph 7 of this Annex (hereinafter 'the trilateral forum'), the Israeli and Palestinian authorities will ensure access to all necessary communication lines and frequencies.

6.   The coordinating body and each observer delegation will have access to either or both of:

a.   special license plates and necessary permits, agreed in the trilateral forum, for cars bought or hired locally; and

b.   special license plates for cars imported and re-exported.

Comprehensive motor insurance shall be acquired for each such car.

7.   Any equipment, materials, articles or goods imported by the coordinating body or any observer delegation in connection with their activities shall be exempt from all custom and import taxes and duties. It is understood, however, that such exemption does not include charges for services provided at Israeli points of entry. In the event of a request to pay storage charges resulting from an undue delay caused by Israeli authorities as certified by the trilateral forum, storage charges shall be reimbursed.

Questions relating to such imports regarding any prohibitions or restrictions in accordance with the law, shall be raised in the trilateral forum and dealt with under expedited procedures.

Each observer delegation will be allowed to import and re-export all equipment, including cars, which it considers necessary to fulfill its duties. Within the framework of the trilateral forum, Israeli and/or Palestinian authorities will perform appropriate customs clearances through a special expedited procedure under the supervision of senior customs officials. All imported equipment, materials, articles or goods exempted from import taxes and duties will be re-exported or donated according to applicable procedures agreed upon between the two sides at the conclusion of the mission of the observer delegations.

8.   a.   Palestinians recruited locally to perform services for the coordinating body or for an observer delegation (hereinafter 'local personnel') shall, subject to the provisions of this paragraph, enjoy in the West Bank and the Gaza Strip:

(1)   freedom of movement in the exercise of their duties; and

(2)   immunity from prosecution in respect of words spoken or written and any act performed by them in the exercise of their duties.

b.   Observer delegations and the coordinating body shall provide lists of local personnel to the CEC, which will accredit such local personnel following prior coordination with Israel. Accredited local personnel shall be issued with a certificate in Arabic, English and Hebrew, possession of which shall be necessary to enjoy the freedom of movement and immunity in subparagraph a. above.

c.   The certificate will include the following text:

'The bearer of this certificate is officially attached to an international observer delegation. He or she is entitled to drive or travel in a vehicle bearing special observer delegation license plates in the course of his or her legitimate duties. He or she is entitled to limited immunity in the course of such duties, in accordance with the Interim Agreement.'

d.   Such local personnel shall not enjoy immunity from any legal process related to traffic offenses, or damage caused by such offences.

e.   Matters regarding arrangements for entry by local personnel into Israel and for movement by local personnel between the West Bank and the Gaza Strip, including the issuance of entry certificates, will be handled within the trilateral forum by the Israeli representative to that forum, who shall, to that end, maintain ongoing contacts with the appropriate Israeli authorities with a view to expediting all related matters.

f.   Local personnel shall not carry arms.

9.   The coordinating body, and observer delegations, may display their flag and/or emblem on their office premises and vehicles.

10.   Within the framework of the trilateral forum, the Palestinian and Israeli authorities will appoint liaison officers as appropriate to ensure that all arrangements relating to requests concerning logistics and security are implemented.

ANNEX 10:

PANAMA: COMMITMENT OF SANTA MARIA LA ANTIGUA

Ethical Electoral Commitment
'Justice and Peace' Commission
Panama, September 1993

The political parties undertake to support and monitor the introduction of a truly democratic system where no one is above the institutions and where all citizens consider themselves represented.

To achieve democracy worthy of its name, the electoral process must be transparent, each must recognise the validity of the results and the parties must accept the outcome of the vote even if it goes against them.

The parties which subscribe to this document stress the need to monitor compliance with the decisions of the Electoral Court. To ensure that this institution is strong and impartial, care must be taken that the influence of the parties or that of the State does not hinder its smooth functioning.

The Electoral Court must enjoy genuine administrative independence so that it functions better and is not subjected to outside pressures which are contrary to its goals.

The political parties undertake to foster the establishment of a culture of dialogue and respect, to refrain from attacking the reputation of other candidates, to forbear from propagating calumnies or rumours about them, and to avoid taking up subjects which touch on their private life. The political parties which aspire to govern the countries must present and debate their ideas and their plan (programmes) so that the voters can take a decision.

The political parties undertake to comply with the time-limit stipulated by the law, which stipulates that any civil servant who wields decision-making power and who wishes to stand for election must first resign. This measure is aimed at preventing candidates from using their office to better their chances of being elected. The time-limit set by the Electoral Court is six months before the date of elections.

The political parties undertake to support the work of the electoral delegates. As their name indicates, these persons represent the Electoral Court and are responsible for participating in and overseeing the electoral process.

The political parties undertake not to use the State as a means of imposing their will. The State must be the political organisation which represents the Nation and serves its interests; it must avoid authoritarianism and see to it that justice is applied and the citizens are respected.

The aim is to take a stand against violence, which must be neither allowed nor provoked, and to advocate wisdom and tolerance. In order to do so, there is a need to avoid physical confrontation and to give up the idea of creating shock troops, armed gangs or private police forces. All conflicts must be settled by the means provided for by the law.

The political parties undertake to respect and ensure respect for the fundamental guarantees (freedom of expression, freedom to elect and to be elected, etc.) so as to ensure that we are all on an equal footing in elections. We hope that all Panamanian citizens will contribute to our struggle for peace and will discharge their civic duty with firmness and dignity.

The parties signatory to this convenant undertake to see to it that the funds, premises, vehicles or other goods of the State are not used by parties or candidates. These goods are the property of all citizens and are needed to cope with the current difficulties which the population is facing.

Any person guilty of the acts described above will be denounced by the political parties which are signatories to this covenant.

Democracy requires that we vote according to our conscience; political parties accordingly undertake not to buy votes by offering money, alcohol, etc. and not to promise appointments – promises which are generally never kept. Schemes of this sort must be condemned for they constitute immoral acts which are harmful to the democratic process.

The political parties promise State officials to fight for the stability of their jobs and call accordingly for the adoption of an "Administrative Career Law" which will protect such officials from any political pressure.

Any civil servant may join the political party of his or her choice without any fear of losing his or her job.

The political parties which sign this covenant undertake to accept the outcome of the election of 8 May and to guarantee a peaceful transition between the former government and the new government in good faith.

ANNEX 11:

CAMBODIA

Code of Conduct 1993

1.   All persons, all political parties, their leaders, members and supporters, all provisionally and officially registered political parties, their leaders, members, supporters and candidates, shall abide by this Code of Conduct.

2.   All political parties are entitled to and shall enjoy, the fundamental right of a free and fair election, including the freedom to campaign.

3.   All political parties shall respect the right and freedom of all other parties to campaign, and disseminate their political ideas and principles without fear.

4.   In particular, all political parties, officially and provisionally registered political parties, their leaders, members, supporters and candidates shall obey the following rules:

(1)   Intimidation, in whatever form, shall be prohibited, and manuals, instructions and orders of political parties and provisionally and officially registered political parties shall reinforce and emphasize this prohibition.

(2)   The possession and use of any weapon of any kind, or of any instrument capable of use as a weapon, at any political rally, meeting, march or demonstration shall be prohibited. Parties' manuals, instructions and orders shall reinforce this prohibition.

(3)   Parties and candidates shall inform the local UNTAC office of any planned public meetings or political rallies, and shall in good faith take all necessary steps to avoid violent confrontation or conflict between their supporters, and shall comply with all directions, instructions or orders issued by UNTAC in relation to such meetings.

(4)   All parties shall avoid the coincidence, in time or place, of their meetings, rallies, marches or demonstrations with those of other parties, and to this end shall liaise and cooperate with UNTAC and with other parties.

(5)   All parties, their members and supporters, shall refrain from disrupting the meetings, marches or demonstrations of other parties.

(6)   Parties and candidates shall at all times avoid, in speeches, broadcasts, pamphlets, newsletters, press statements, posters, their party platforms, campaign advertisements or otherwise, using inflammatory language or other language which threatens or incites violence in any form against others.

(7)   All political parties shall refrain from obstructing persons from attending the meetings, marches or rallies of other parties.

(8)   All parties shall refrain from plagiarising the symbols of other parties, and shall not steal, destroy or disfigure the political or other campaign material or posters of other parties, or the election information material of UNTAC.

(9)   All political parties, and especially their leaders, shall ensure freedom of access of other parties to all potential voters on public or private property, in camps or

reception centres, or wherever they may be. Parties shall ensure that potential voters wishing to participate in political activities are free to do so.

(10) All parties shall consistently reinforce and emphasize to their supporters and to all voters that the ballot will be secret, and that no person will know how any individual has voted.

(11) All parties shall establish effective communication with one another at the central, provincial and district levels, and shall appoint liaison personnel, to be available for this purpose at all times, to deal with any problem arising during registration of voters, the campaign or the polling.

(12) All parties shall attend at least once every two weeks a meeting under the chairmanship of the Chief Electoral Officer to discuss any matters of concern relating to the campaign. In addition, a standing committee of leaders of registered political parties shall attend at least every two weeks a meeting under the chairmanship of the Special Representative or his deputy to deal with matters of concern relating to the campaign. The above-mentioned meetings shall commence from a date to be determined by the Special Representative.

(13) All parties shall bring all information or complaints regarding intimidation or other allegations of unlawful conduct immediately to the attention of UNTAC.

(14) Parties shall not abuse the right to complain, nor make false, frivolous or vexatious complaints.

(15) All parties shall cooperate fully with the Special Representatives's Electoral Advisory Committee.

(16) All parties shall issue instructions and orders to their members and supporters to observe the Electoral Law, this Code, the instructions of UNTAC officials, and all orders and directives of the Special Representative, and take all necessary steps in good faith to ensure compliance with the Electoral Law and this Code.

(17) The Special Representative and all parties shall publicize this Code and the electoral law throughout Cambodia by all means at their disposal.

ANNEX 12:

GHANA

**Code of Conduct
for Political Parties in Ghana for Public Elections**

The Registered Political Parties of Ghana realising the need for a Code of Conduct for their activities during public elections hereby make this Code of Conduct which shall be adhered to by all political parties:

1.   Existing election laws and rules must be complied with by all political parties.

2.   All political parties and contestants shall extend all necessary help and co-operation to the law-enforcing authorities.

3.   Everyone should not only be aware of his rights, but should also respect the rights of others.

4.   All political parties and candidates participating in the polls shall extend full co-operation to the election officials and ensure their safety and security before, during and after the polls.

5.   Election campaigns should be so organised that a congenial and peaceful atmosphere prevails during polling.

6.   The political parties shall not propagate any opinion, or action which in any manner is prejudicial to the sovereignty, integrity or security of Ghana, or the maintenance of public order, or the integrity or independence of the judiciary of Ghana or which defies or brings into ridicule the judiciary or the armed forces of Ghana, or which is immoral.

7.   The political parties, their candidates, agents or workers shall not obstruct or break up meetings organised by rival parties and candidates, nor interrupt speeches or prevent distribution of handbills, leaflets and pasting of posters of other parties and candidates and shall not destroy or deface posters of other parties.

8.   Political parties shall avoid criticism of other political parties, their leaders and candidates on matters that have no bearing an their public activities. Criticism and comments shall be confined to policies and programmes of the parties. Speeches and slogans shall be dignified and based on principles of morality, decorum and decency.

9.   Political parties shall refrain from speeches calculated to arouse parochial feelings and controversy or conflicts between sects, communities and ethnic groups.

10.   Public leaders and all other participants in political activity shall act with a sense or responsibility and dignity benefitting their status. While propagating their own views and programmes, they shall not interfere with the freedom of others to do the same as that would be the negation of democracy.

11.   Appeals to violence or resort to violence during meetings, processions, or during polling hours shall be strictly avoided.

12. Carriage of dangerous and lethal weapons shall not be allowed in public meetings and official regulations in this regard shall be strictly observed. Use of fire crackers and other explosives at public meetings shall not be allowed.

13. Political parties and their candidates shall extend co-operation to the officers on election duty in order to ensure peaceful and orderly polling and complete freedom for the voters to exercise their franchise without being subject to any annoyance or obstruction.

14. Political parties and their candidates shall scrupulously avoid all activities which amount to 'corrupt practices' and offences under the electoral laws; such as bribing of voters, intimidation of voters, impersonation of voters, canvassing within 500 metres of a polling station.

15. Political parties, their candidates, agents or workers shall not indulge in offering gifts or gratification or inducing another to stand or not to stand as a candidate, or to withdraw or not to withdraw his candidature.

16. Political parties and their candidates shall not procure the support or assistance of any public servant or official of the Electoral Commission to promote or hinder the election of a candidate.

17. Political parties and their candidates should not procure the support of sympathizers to destroy ballot paper or any official mark on the ballot paper.

18. Notwithstanding any of the above, all political parties shall be vocal against violence. No party shall give indulgence to any kind of violent activity to demonstrate parry strength or to prove supremacy. All political parties will extend co-operation to the law enforcing agencies for recovery of illegal arms. No party shall take any initiative for the release of any person arrested by police with arms during election campaign or in the polling centre during voting or in the vicinity of the polling centre during polls.

19. Assistance of the nearest law-enforcing agencies, namely, the police, Ghana Armed Forces, the Fire Service and the Prison Services shall be sought to resist and check any election offence.

20. Political parties will reach an understanding to resist attempts to procure votes by forcible occupation of polling centres or illegal activities in the polling centres, by any person. Votes thus obtained illegally will be of no use as the Electoral Commission will cancel polling in such centres.

21. The congenial and peaceful atmosphere for election must not be disturbed by spreading untrue and motivated rumour or by taking recourse to conspiracy.

22. On the declaration of a free and fair election by the Commission to the satisfaction of the majority of the political parties, invited persons and recognised observers, losing candidates will honourably concede defeat.

For this Code of Conduct to enjoy maximum respect by the agents and supporters of the political parties, it must be seen to be endorsed by all the presidential candidates and all the chairpersons of the political parties.

To this end, this Code shall be launched by the Electoral Commission together with all the Presidential Candidates contesting the 1992 elections and the Chairpersons of the political parties.

Made at Accra 23rd day of October, 1992.

ANNEX 13:

GUYANA

Guidelines for Media and Political Parties

1.   Contextual Background

Freedom of expression by the media — radio, television and print — is a symbol of democracy. The manner in which the media use their freedom carries an obligation to serve the society and public as a whole. Because of this need to serve the public, the media inherit a public trust. The media have a responsibility to conduct their operations at all times in a professional manner and to exercise critical and discerning judgment which respects and advances the rights and dignity of all people and maintains standards of good taste as reflected by the society and public served. The media must enrich the daily life of the people they serve through information, education and entertainment; they must provide for the fair discussion of matters of public concern; engage in works directed toward the common good; and volunteer aid and comfort in times of stress and emergency.

2.   General Guidelines during the Campaign Period[258]

(a)   News

News reporting should be factual, fair and without bias. Professional care should be maintained in the use and selection of news sources. News analysis, commentary and editorials should be clearly identified as such, distinguishing them from straight news reporting.

(b)   Controversial Public Issues

Expressions of responsible views on public issues of a controversial nature should give fair representation to opposing sides of issues. Requests by individuals, groups or organizations to present their views on controversial public issues should be considered on the basis of their individual merits and in the light of their contributions to the public interest.

3.   Specific Guidelines for the Campaign Period

(a)   Access by Political Parties

During the Campaign Period, the media have a special responsibility to the public to encourage participation by the electorate in the democratic process and to ensure they have the opportunity to be informed on the candidates and issues. To enable this, the

---

[258]   The official campaign period for these Guidelines is defined as that time between Nomination Day and Election Day.

Guyana Elections Commission requests that the broadcast media — radio and television — make available at no cost a minimum of five minutes of prime time weekly to each political party with candidates for national office, and also requests that daily publication print media make available at no cost 10 column inches of space weekly to each qualified political party. The Chairman of the Elections Commission shall notify the media of the Parties that qualify for this free coverage. All such programs and columns should be clearly identified as a public service political message prepared by the (name) political party and unedited by the (media). The (name) political party is solely responsible for its content. Programs and messages exceeding the free time and space allocations may be rejected or returned to the Party. The media may establish reasonable deadlines for submission of the materials in order to fit their broadcast or publication schedules. The media shall ensure all Parties are given equal treatment and access as to time and location of these messages. Concerning access to radio broadcasts, in order to provide complete geographic coverage, it may be necessary to repeat the programs at a different time and frequency.

(b)   Paid Political Messages

Political parties or candidates who wish additional time and space should pay for all messages or advertisements at current established rates — preferably the lowest published rate — but each Party should be charged the same rate.

Further the media must ensure that all Parties and candidates have equal access to the broadcast times and schedule for broadcast media; and similar equitable access, space and location, for print media. One political Party or candidate should not be allowed to block access by other Parties or candidates by purchasing all availabilities of time or space.

Equitable and fair treatment of all Parties and candidates must be the standard adhered to by all media. While the above addresses equitable treatment concerning broadcast or publication of the messages, the same standard must be applied to any production in preparation for broadcast or publication.

Payment terms for political advertisements should be the same for all Parties utilizing the industry standard of cash in advance. All paid political messages should carry a statement that they are a 'Paid Political Advertisement'.

(c)   Correction of Media Errors

Broadcast or publication errors beyond the control of the medium, i.e. mechanical failure or act of God, should be corrected in accordance with the standard broadcast or publication policies of procedures for the correction of mistakes. The media may not censor, change or alter in any manner any of the materials presented by the Parties or candidates for broadcast or publication by the media.

(d)   Questionable Materials

In the event any of the media believe a political message may not be in good taste, or contrary to the public interest, security, peace or morality, the questioned political message may be rejected by the media. However the media must provide specific details to the Party as to the reason for rejection and allow the material to be changed to meet broadcast or publication standards.

(e) Disclaimers

The media shall insert or broadcast a disclaimer daily when any free or paid political messages will be carried published by their medium. For example: 'The political messages or advertisements published in today's newspaper are prepared by the Political Party or candidate without editing or change and do not necessarily reflect the opinion of this newspaper.' One insert anywhere in the newspaper should be sufficient. A similar statement shall be made by the broadcast media at least once during the broadcast day and not necessarily immediately preceding or following broadcast of political material.

ANNEX 14:

SEYCHELLES

Code of Conduct to be Adhered to by Political Parties, their Members and Supporters on an Election or Referendum

This Code of Conduct is aimed at maintaining a peaceful atmosphere during an election or referendum campaign and on polling day.

Code of Conduct

1.   Existing election laws and rules must be adhered to.

2.   All political parties and contestants will have to extend all necessary help and co-operation to the law-enforcing authorities.

3.   Everyone should be aware not only of his own rights, but should also respect the rights of others.

4.   All political parties and candidates participating in the polls will extend full co-operation to election officials and ensure their safety until the polls are over.

5.   Election campaigns should be so organised that a congenial and peaceful atmosphere prevails during polling.

6.   It is expected that criticism of opponents will occur during electioneering. All parties shall exercise restraint in speech, manner and conduct, and show respect for the opinion of others so that electioneering does not turn into a war of words and confrontation.

7.   It is expected that criticism of opponents will occur during electioneering. However, indecorous and provocative speeches, statements, posters, taunting, ridiculing and innuendoes shall be avoided. Parties shall be careful so that behaviour, statements or comments do not cause unnecessary tension.

8.   All political parties shall be vocal against violence. No party shall give indulgence to any kind of violent activity to demonstrate party strength or to prove supremacy. All political parties will extend co-operation to the law-enforcing agencies for recovery of illegal arms. No party will take any initiative for the release of any person arrested by police with arms during an election or referendum campaign or in the polling station during voting or in the vicinity of the polling station during polls.

9.   All parties and candidates will have equal opportunity for publicity. Meetings, processions and other campaign activities of opponents cannot be interfered with. Posters and banners shall be displayed only in accordance with the Code of Conduct set out in the Schedule hereto.

10.   Assistance of the nearest law-enforcing agencies will have to be sought to resist and check any sort of election offence.

11.   Any attempts to influence voting through money or allurement are election offences. Everyone should be aware of these offences.

12.   No Government transport shall be used to carry voters to polling stations other than persons working for Government departments who are on duty or persons living in Government institutions. This rule does not apply to a person who has the use of a Government vehicle and the vehicle is used for self and family.

13.   No Defence Force vehicles shall be used to carry voters, including Defence Force personnel, to polling stations.

14.   Defence Force personnel shall not go to vote in their uniform.

15.   Political parties will not procure votes by forcible occupation of polling stations or through illegal activities in the polling stations.

16.   No candidate or party can commit or give covertly or overtly any contribution, grant or favour to any individual, institution, body or organization until election or referendum day for the purpose of election campaigning and obtaining votes.

17.   The congenial and peaceful atmosphere for an election or a referendum cannot be disturbed by spreading untrue and motivated rumour or by having recourse to conspiracy.

18.   No election camps, check points and refreshment stalls shall be set up by political parties, their members and supporters. There shall be no campaigning of any sort either individually or collectively on polling day. District Council offices shall be closed on the day of the election or referendum. Voters must be left alone when queuing up so that they are not influenced in any way.

19.   Where a voter is incapacitated by blindness or other physical cause or otherwise, he may ask the Electoral Officer to record his vote in the presence of a person selected by him. In those circumstances the Electoral Officer shall satisfy himself that: (a) the voter is truly incapacitated as he claims to be; (b) that the person who is to witness the vote has been freely and genuinely chosen by the voter; and (c) that the vote expressed by the voter is free. In this respect the political parties shall not abuse this procedure to pressure incapacitated persons to vote in their favour.

20.   In addition to election officials, only the voters are entitled to enter the 'polling stations.' The political parties shall make sure that their workers do not enter the polling stations and loiter therein. Only the polling and counting agents will remain seated at their designated seats in the polling station and discharge their responsibility from there. No disruption shall be caused by the moving or changing of accredited agents.

Code of Conduct Relating to Posters and Banners

1.0   Use of Bulletin Boards

1.1   Any elections or referendum notice, political advertisement or announcement shall be displayed only on bulletin boards.

1.2   These bulletin boards or hoardings will be erected only at certain specific places agreed upon by the Land Transport Division, Police (Traffic Section) and Planning Authority.

1.3   The Planning Authority, Police (Traffic Section) and Land Transport Division shall agree on the size, height and number of the boards to be displayed in a particular area.

1.4 The Department of Tourism and Transport (Tourism Division) has already erected some permanent bill boards in Victoria. Only advertisements announcing local events such as educational, cultural, social or recreational and tourism-promoting activities should be displayed on these boards.

1.5 Extra bulletin boards (temporary) may be erected and allocated to the different political parties.

1.6 Boards will be erected only 14 days prior to the day of the election or referendum.

1.7 All boards and political displays must be removed by the political parties as soon as possible, in any case within 14 days of the close of the poll in the election or referendum in accordance with regulation 13 (2) (b) of the Town and Country Planning (Control of Advertisements) Regulations, Cap 160.

2.0 Use of Cloth Banners

2.1 Easily removable cloth banners should be utilised as much as possible instead of pasted paper posters.

2.2 Cloth banners shall be displayed only after the necessary permission has been obtained from the Land Transport Division and Police (Traffic Section).

2.3 All banners shall be removed as soon as possible, in any case, within 14 days after the election or referendum.

3.0 Use of Paint

3.1 There shall be a total ban on the use of paint (liquids and sprays) to write upon, mark or paint any slogan on any road, pavement, telephone or electric posts, wall, or fence, etc., whether on public or private property.

This is an offence punishable under Section 183 (j) of the Penal Code, Cap 73.

4.0 Electoral or Referendum Posters

4.1 Electoral or Referendum posters shall be affixed only on special boards erected for this purpose as set out in paragraph 1.

4.2 No poster or any other paper shall be pasted on any wall, building, road, pavement, telephone or electric poles, or fence whether public or private property.

This is an offence punishable under Section 183 (j) of the Penal Code, Cap 73.

5.0 Respect of Others and their Property

5.1 Political party members and supporters shall respect others and their property and shall refrain from causing damage to any property whether public or private.

ANNEX 15:

BANGLADESH

Code of Conduct to be Adhered to by Political Parties
Jatiya Sangsad (Parliament) Election, 1991

The code of conduct, finalised after discussions with the representatives of 67 political parties including major ones, is aimed at maintaining a peaceful atmosphere during the election campaign and on polling day. The Election Commission hoped that if all political parties faithfully abide by the code, they would greatly contribute to the holding of a credible election in the country. Legitimacy of a representative government elected through such an election will not be questioned.

Code of Conduct

1. Existing election laws and rules must be adhered to.

2. All political parties and contestants will have to extend all necessary help and co-operation to the law-enforcing authorities.

3. Everyone should be aware of not only his own rights, but should also respect the rights of others.

4. All political parties and candidates participating in the polls will extend full co-operation to the election officials and ensure their safety and security until the polls are over.

5. Election campaigns should be so organised that a congenial and peaceful atmosphere prevails during polling.

6. Nothing should be done that will create tension and disrupt the congenial atmosphere of the election. All parties should exercise restraint in speech and show respect to the opinions of others so that electioneering does not turn into war of words.

7. It is expected that criticism of opponents will occur during electioneering. However, indecorous and provocative speeches/statements, taunting, ridiculing and innuendos should be avoided. Parties should be careful so that statements or comments do not cause unnecessary tension. In case a situation for the possibility of a clash arises because of a misunderstanding between contesting parties, then an Election Co-ordination Committee composed of representatives from the concerned parties shall allay tension and settle the dispute.

8. All political parties shall be vocal against violence. No party shall give indulgence to any kind of violent activity to demonstrate party strength or to prove supremacy. All political parties will extend co-operation to the law enforcing agencies for recovery of illegal arms. No party will take any initiative for the release of any person arrested by police with arms during election campaign or in the polling centre during voting or in the vicinity of the polling centre during polls.

9. All parties and candidates will have equal opportunity for publicity. Meetings, processions and other campaign activities of opponents cannot be interfered with.

10.   Assistance of the nearest law enforcing agencies will have to be sought to resist and check any sort of election offence.

11.   Any attempts to influence voting through money or allurement and to hire or use any kind of transport to carry voters other than for self and family are election offences. Everyone should be aware of these offences.

12.   Political parties will reach an understanding to resist attempts to procure votes by forcible occupation of polling centres or thorough illegal activities in the polling centres. Votes thus obtained illegally will be of no use as the Election Commission will cancel polling in such centres.

13.   No candidate can commit covertly or overtly any contribution or grant to any institution in his constituency until election day for the purpose of election campaigning and obtaining votes.

14.   The congenial and peaceful atmosphere for election can not be disturbed by spreading untrue and motivated rumour or by taking recourse to conspiracy.

15.   Election camps cannot be set up within the prohibited area or close to the polling centres and no campaign shall be allowed inside the polling centres.

16.   In addition to the election officials, only the voters are entitled to enter the polling centres: the political parties should make sure that their workers do not enter the polling centres and loiter therein. Only the polling agents will remain seated at their designated seats in the polling centre and discharge their responsibility from there.

ANNEX 16:

OSCE: ELECTION OBSERVATION CODE OF CONDUCT[259]

- Observers will carry the prescribed identification issued by the host government or election commission, and will identify themselves to any interested authority upon request.

- Observers will maintain strict impartiality in the conduct of their duties, and shall at no time express any bias or preference in relation to national authorities, parties, candidates, or with reference to any issues in contention in the election process.

- Observers will not display or wear any partisan symbols, colours, or banners.

- Observers will undertake their duties in an unobtrusive manner, and will not interfere with the election process, polling day procedures, or the vote count.

- Observers may wish to bring irregularities to the attention of the local election officials, but they must never give instructions or countermand decision of the elections officials.

- Observers will base all conclusions on well-documented, factual, and verifiable evidence.

- Observers will refrain from making any personal or premature comments about their observations to the media or any other interested persons, and will limit any remarks to general information about the nature of their activity as observers.

- Observers will participate in post-election debriefings, by fax or telephone if necessary.

- Observers must comply with all national laws and regulations.

---

[259] OSCE, *The OSCE/ODIHR Election Observation Handbook*, Warsaw, 2nd ed., 1997, 5-6.

Select Bibliography

Agenda for Change. The Report of the Hansard Society Commission on Election Campaigns. Hansard Society, London, 1991.

Alexander, Herbert E. & Corrado, Anthony, *Financing the 1992 Election,* M.E. Sharpe, Armonk, WY, 1995; reviewed by Sharon Steward in *The Guardian* (Journal of the Council on Governmental Ethics Laws—COGEL), Mar. 1996, 1-3.

Ansolabehere, Stephen & Iyengar, Shanto, *Going Negative: How Political Advertisements Shrink and Polarize the Electorate,* The Free Press, New York, NY, 1995; reviewed by Maris LeBlanc McCrory, *The Guardian* (Journal of the Council on Governmental Ethics Laws—COGEL), Dec. 1996, 1,3.

Axworthy, T., 'Capital Intensive Politics', in Seidle, F. Leslie, ed., *Issues in Party and Election Finance in Canada,* Research Studies of the Royal Commission on Electoral Reform and Party Financing, 5, Toronto, Dundurn Press, 1991.

Baldwin, R., *Rules and Government,* Clarendon Press, Oxford, 1995

Balz, D. & Edsall, T.B., 'More Shouts and Smears as the Querulous Republicans Debate', *International Herald Tribune,* 2-3 Mar. 1996

Beibeder, Yves, *International Monitoring of Plebiscites, Referenda and National Elections.* Dordrecht, Martinus Nijhoff, 1994.

Bennet, J., 'Who's Negative? Check Clinton Ads', *International Herald Tribune,* 23 Oct. 1996.

Berke, R.L., 'Attack Ads Arouse Anger', *International Herald Tribune,* 17-18 Feb. 1996

Boutros-Ghali, Boutros, 'Support by the United Nations System of the Efforts of Governments to Promote and Consolidate New or Restored Democracies': UN doc. A/51/761, 20 Dec. 1996; re-issued as *An Agenda for Democratization,* United Nations, New York. 1996

Brownlie, I., *System of the Law of Nations: State Responsibility (Part I),* Clarendon Press, Oxford. 1983.

Brownlie, I., *Principles of Public International Law,* Clarendon Press, Oxford. 4th ed. 1990.

Bulgarian Association for Fair Elections and Civil Rights, 'Mirror', The Race for the Presidential Post mirrored in the Media, 2 issues, Oct., Nov. 1996.

Camby, Jean-Pierre, *Le financement de la vie politique en France,* Montchrestien, Paris, 1995.

Cantor, Joseph E.,'Campaign Financing in Federal Elections: A Guide to the Law and its Operation,' Congressional Research Service (CRS) Report for Congress, 8 Aug. 1986; updated 15 Oct. 1993.

Carville, J. & Matalin, M., *All's Fair: Love, War and Running for President,* Random House, 1994. Touchstone, 1995.

Center for Responsive Politics, Washington, D.C., 'Enforcing the Campaign Finance Laws: An Agency Model', June 1993.

Commonwealth Observer Group, *The General Election in St. Kitts and Nevis, 3 July 1995,* Commonwealth Secretariat, London, 1996.

Commonwealth Observer Group, *The Parliamentary Elections in Bangladesh, 12 June 1996*, Commonwealth Secretariat, London, 1997.

Commonwealth Observer Group, *The Presidential and Parliamentary Elections in Sierra Leone, 26-27 February 1996,* Commonwealth Secretariat, London, 1996.

Commonwealth Observer Group, *The General Election in Pakistan, 3 February 1997,* London, 1997, 2.

Commonwealth Observer Group, *The Union Presidential and Parliamentary Elections in Tanzania, 29 October 1995,* Commonwealth Secretariat, London, 1996.

Conseil fédéral de la Suisse, 'Rapport sur l'aide aux partis politiques', 23 nov. 1988 (doc. 88.075).

Cooper, L. & Henderson, J., 'Uganda: A Pre-Election Assessment Report', International Federation for Election Systems, Washington, D.C. Jan. 1996,

Cornillon, P., 'Rights and Responsibilities of Election Observers', paper presented to the International Conference in La Laguna on Freedom of Elections and the International Observation of Elections (Tenerife, 27 Feb.- 2 March 1994).

Council on Governmental Ethics Laws (COGEL), 'A Model Law for Campaign Finance, Ethics and Lobbying Regulation', (1991).

Council of Europe, *Handbook for Observers of Elections,* Strasbourg. 1996.

DeGregorio, Paul S. & Ross, Kimberly L., 'Albania: Pre-Election Technical Assessment', International Federation for Election Systems, Washington, D.C. Aug. 1996.

Doublet, Yves-Marie, 'La législation de 1995 sur le financement de la vie politique', *Revue française de droit constitutionnel,* no. 22, 1995, 411.

Durbin, Thomas M., 'Extending the Fairness Doctrine to the Print Media', Congressional Research Service Report for Congress, 17 Jun. 1987.

Durbin, Thomas M., 'First Amendment Issues and Major Supreme Court Decisions relating to Campaign Finance Law', Congressional Research Service Report for Congress, updated 15 Sept. 1995.

Elections Canada, *Election Handbook for Candidates, their Official Agents and Auditors,* Ottawa, 1993.

Elections Canada, *Thirty-fifth General Election 1993. Contributions and Expenses of Registered Political Parties and Candidates,* Ottawa, 1994

Elections Canada, *Serving Democracy,* Ottawa, 1994.

Elections Canada, *Contributions and Expenses of Registered Political Parties and Candidates, 35th General Election 1993,* Ottawa, 1993.

Elections Canada, *Strengthening the Foundation: Canada's Electoral System,* Annex to the Report of the Chief Electoral Officer of Canada on the 35th General Election, Ottawa, 1996.

European Institute for the Media, 'Preliminary conclusions—Media coverage of the Russian presidential elections', 17 Jun. 1996.

Ewing, Keith D., *Money, Politics and Law: A Study of Electoral Campaign Finance Reform in Canada,* Clarendon Press, Oxford, 1992.

Franck, T., 'The Emerging Right to Democratic Governance', 86 *American Journal of International Law* 46 (1992)

Gallagher M. & Marsh, M., eds., *Candidate Selection in Comparative Perspective. The Secret Garden of Politics,* Sage Modern Politics Series, vol. 18, 1988.

Gans, Curtis, Committee for the Study of the American Electorate, Evidence to the US Senate Subcommittee on Communications on the *Clean Campaign Act*, May 1993.

Garber, Larry, 'The Role of International Observers', in Garber, L. & Bjornlund, E., eds., *The New Democratic Frontier. A Country by Country Report on Elections In Central and Eastern Europe,* National Democratic Institute for International Affairs, Washington, D.C. 1992.

Garber, Larry, *Guidelines for International Election Observing,* International Human Rights Law Group, 1983.

Garber, Larry and Gibson, Clark, *Review of United Nations Electoral Assistance 1992-93*, Aug. 1993.

Garber, L. & Bjornlund, E., eds., *The New Democratic Frontier. A Country by Country Report on Elections In Central and Eastern Europe,* National Democratic Institute for International Affairs, Washington, D.C. 1992.

Genevois, Bruno, 'Le nouveau rôle du juge de l'élection', in 'L'argent des élections', *Pouvoirs,* No. 70, 1994, 69.

Goodwin-Gill, G.S., *Free and Fair Elections: International Law and Practice,* Inter-Parliamentary Union, Geneva, 1994.

Gould, R., Jackson, C. & Wells, L., *Strengthening Democracy: A Parliamentary Perspective,* Dartmouth, Aldershot, 1995.

Gugliotta, Guy & Chinoy, Ira, 'Money-Machine: The Fund-Raising Frenzy of Campaign '96. Outsiders Made Erie Battle a National Battle', *Washington Post,* 10 Feb. 1997.

Human Rights Committee, 'General Comment adopted by the Human Rights Committee under Article 40, Paragraph 4, of the International Covenant on Civil and Political Rights', Addendum, 'General Comment No. 25 (57)': UN doc. CCPR/C/21/Rev.1/Add.7, 27 Aug. 1996

Human Rights Watch/Helsinki, 'Statement of Concern: Violations in the Albanian Elections', 30 May 1996.

Human Rights Watch, 'Leaving Human Rights Behind: The Context of the Presidential Elections', 16 May 1997.

Human Rights Watch, 'Algeria-Elections in the Shadow of Violence and Repression,' 20 May 1997.

International Federation for Election Systems (IFES), 'Republic of Moldova Presidential Elections, November 17 and December 1, 1996', Washington, D.C. 1997.

IFES, *Europe and Asia Report,* Washington, D.C. Feb. 1997.

IFES, 'Republic of Georgia: Assessment and Voter Education Campaign, September-November 1995', Washington, D.C. Nov. 1996.

IFES, 'Toward Credible and Legitimate Elections in Kenya: Recommendations for Action', Apr. 1996.

IFES, 'Albania: A Pre-Election Technical Assessment', Washington, D.C. Aug. 1996.

IFES, 'Uganda: A Pre-Election Assessment Report', Washington, D.C. Jan. 1996.

Inter-Parliamentary Union, Declaration on Criteria for Free and Fair Elections, Inter-Parliamentary Council, 154th session, Paris, 26 March 1994

Inter-Parliamentary Union, Specialized Inter-Parliamentary Conference, 'Towards Partnership between Men and Women in Politics', New Delhi, 14-18 Feb. 1997, Concluding Statement by the President on the Outcome of the Conference.

International Crisis Group, 'Electioneering in Republika Srpska', ICG Bosnia Project, Sarajevo, Aug. 1996.

International Crisis Group, Press Release, 4 Dec. 1996, 'ICG Cautions Against Further Electoral Engineering in the Run-up to the Municipal Elections'.

International Crisis Group, 'Elections in Bosnia & Herzegovina,' Sarajevo, 22 Sept. 1996.

International Crisis Group, 'Elections in Bosnia and Herzegovina', Sarajevo, 13 Aug. 1996.

International IDEA, 'Lessons learnt: International Election Observation', Report on a Roundtable, Stockholm, 10-12 Oct. 1995.

Jones, George F., 'Fraud and Corruption in Elections and Election Campaigns', Address to the Seminar on Public Ethics sponsored by the Ministry of the Interior, Republic of Argentina, Buenos Aires, 10 Dec. 1996.

Kalb, D. & Salant, J.D., 'Donations by Pro-Israel PACs in Decline on Capitol Hill', *Congressional Quarterly,* 16 Mar. 1996, 719; '1995 Campaign Finance Totals', *Congressional Quarterly,* 6 Apr. 1996, 954;

Klein, Keith, 'Election Observation in Tanzania: An Observer Asks if the Task is Too Great', *Elections Today,* Vol. 5, No. 4, Jan. 1996.

Klein, K., Scallan, A., Santos de Assunçao, C. & Dauphinais, D., 'Toward Credible and Legitimate Elections in Kenya: Recommendations for Action', IFES, Washington, D.C. Apr. 1996.

Koenig, Pierre, 'Funding of political parties', Study prepared for the Council of Europe: CE doc. CAHDD(94)45, 20 Sept. 1994, 4-5.

Kurtz, H., 'The Man behind the Voices that Keep Shrieking "Liberal",' *International Herald Tribune,* 23 Oct. 1996.

Lansell, S.R. & Edgeworth, L.V., 'Republic of Georgia: Assessment and Voter Education Campaign, September-November 1995', International Federation for Election Systems, Washington, D.C. Nov. 1996.

Linton, M., *Money and Votes,* Institute for Public Policy Research, London, 1994.

Manin, Bernard, *The Principles of Representative Government,* Cambridge University Press, Cambridge. 1997.

Marcus, Ruth & Babcock, Charles R., 'The System Cracks under the Weight of Cash: Candidates, Parties and Outside Interests Dropped a Record $2.7 Billion', *Washington Post,* 9 Feb. 1997.

McNair, Lord *The Law of Treaties,* Clarendon Press, Oxford. 1961

Merloe, Patrick, 'Electoral Operations, Human Rights and Public Confidence in a Democratic System', National Democratic Institute, Washington, D.C., 1994.

Merloe, Patrick, 'Electoral Campaigns and Pre-Election Issues: The "Level Playing Field" and Democratic Elections', National Democratic Institute, Washington, D.C., 1994.

Merloe, P., *Election Campaign Broadcasting in Transitional Democracies: Problems, Principles and Guidelines*, Article 19, London. 1994.

Millon, Charles, 'Avant/après: Ce qui a changé', in 'L'argent des élections', *Pouvoirs,* No. 70, 1994, 103.

National Democratic Institute (NDI), Press Release, 'Preliminary Statement by the International Observer Delegation to the December 7 Elections in Ghana', Accra, 10 Dec. 1996.

NDI, Statement of the National Democratic Institute for International Affairs (NDI), Pre-Election Assessment Delegation, Accra, 19 Nov. 1996.

National Democratic Institute for International Affairs and The Carter Center, 'Statement of the Second NDI/Carter Center Pre-Election Delegation to the 1996 Palestinian Elections', 16 Dec. 1995.

NDI/Council of Freely Elected Heads of Government Delegation to the Dominican Republic, May 1996, Press Release, Carter Center, Atlanta, 10 May 1996.

Nicholson, B., 'From interest group to (almost) equal citizenship: Women's representation in the Norwegian Parliament', 46 *Parliamentary Affairs* 254 (1993).

Norwegian Helsinki Committee, Report on the Russian Presidential Elections 1996.

Norwegian Helsinki Committee, *Manual for Election Observation,* (Rev. March 1996)

Office for Democratic Institutions and Human Rights (ODIHR), *Final Report,* Romanian Parliamentary and Presidential Elections, 3rd and 17th November 1996.

Office for Democratic Institutions and Human Rights, *Final Report,* Bulgarian Presidential Election, October 27 and November 3, 1996.

Office for Democratic Institutions and Human Rights, 'What Observers need to know about Election Administration', 'The Pre-Election Phase', and 'Election Phase: The Long- and Short-Term Observer', papers presented to the Organization for Cooperation and Security in Europe/Office for Democratic Institutions and Human Rights Seminar on Election Administration and Election Observation, Warsaw, 8-10 Apr. 1997.

Office for Democratic Institutions and Human Rights, *Final Report,* Armenian Presidential Election, September 22, 1996.

Organization for Cooperation and Security in Europe, Press Release, 'Election Appeals Sub-Commission Announces Decisions', 24 Aug. 1996

Organization for Cooperation and Security in Europe Parliamentary Assembly, Stockholm Declaration, 9 July 1996

Organization for Cooperation and Security in Europe, Mission to Bosnia and Herzegovina, Press Release, 24 Aug. 1996.

Organization for Cooperation and Security in Europe, Mission to Bosnia and Herzegovina, Press Release, 15 Aug. 1996.

Organization for Cooperation and Security in Europe, 'The Elections in Bosnia and Herzegovina, 14 September 1996,' Preliminary Statement of the Co-ordinator for International Monitoring (CIM), 16 Sept. 1996.

Organization for Cooperation and Security in Europe, 'Report on the Election of the President of the Russian Federation, 16 June and 3 July 1996'

Organization for Cooperation and Security in Europe, Mission to Bosnia and Herzegovina, Provisional Election Commission, Rules and Regulations. Decisions until July 16, 1996.

Organization for Cooperation and Security in Europe, Press Release, 'Election Appeals Sub-Commission: Decisions taken in two cases of violations of voters' rights', 15 Aug. 1996.

Organization for Cooperation and Security in Europe/Office for Democratic Institutions and Human Rights, *The Organization for Cooperation and Security in Europe/Office for Democratic Institutions and Human Rights Election Observation Handbook,* 2nd ed., 1997.

Organization for Cooperation and Security in Europe, Parliamentary Assembly, Report on the parliamentary elections in Albania, 26 May 1996.

Organization of American States, Unit for the Promotion of Democracy, 'Establishment of the Electoral Observer Mission of the Organization of American States', 1995.

Organization of American States, Unit for the Promotion of Democracy, Final Report of the OAS Electoral Observation Mission to the Legislative and Municipal Elections in Haiti 1995.

Paige Whitaker, L., 'Political Broadcasting Laws and the Indecency Standard: The Issue of Campaign Advertisements Featuring Dead Fetuses and Abortion Procedures', Congressional Research Service Report for Congress, 14 Jul. 1993.

Palestinian Centre for Human Rights and Robert F. Kennedy Memorial Centre for Human Rights, 'Joint Statement regarding Human Rights and Palestinian Elections', 19 Jan. 1996.

Pedersen, M.N. and Bille, 'Public Financing and Public Control of Political Parties in Denmark', in Wiberg, Matti, *The Public Purse and Political Parties. Political Financing of Political Parties in Nordic Countries.* Finnish Political Science Association. 1991.

Pianin, Eric, 'Money-Machine: The Fund-Raising Frenzy of Campaign '96. How Business Found Benefits in Wage Bill', *Washington Post,* 11 Feb. 1997

Poland: National Electoral Office, 'Polish Electoral Law: A Brief Outline,' paper submitted to the Organization for Cooperation and Security in Europe/ Office for Democratic Institutions and Human Rights Seminar on Election Administration and Election Observation, Warsaw, 8-10 Apr. 1997.

Reeves, P.R., '1996 Presidential Elections in Equatorial Guinea', International Federation for Election Systems, Washington, D.C. Mar. 1996, 43

Rotberg, Robert I., 'Democracy in Africa: The Ballot doesn't Tell All', *Christian Science Monitor,* 1 May 1996.

Salant, J., 'Freshmen Embrace Capitol Ways as They Go for PAC Donations', *Congressional Quarterly,* 20 Apr. 1996, 1068

Seidle, F. Leslie, ed., *Issues in Party and Election Finance in Canada,* Research Studies of the Royal Commission on Electoral Reform and Party Financing, 5, Toronto, Dundurn Press, 1991.

Sterline, B., 'Merchants of Venom', *Wired,* May 1996, 65.

United Nations General Assembly (UNGA) res. 50/87 (18 Dec. 1995), 'Cooperation between the United Nations and the Organization for Security and Cooperation in Europe'.

UNGA res. 50/158 (21 Dec. 1995), 'Cooperation between the United Nations and the Organization of African Unity'.

UNGA res. 50/172 (22 Dec. 1995), 'Respect for the principles of national sovereignty and non-interference in the internal affairs of States in their electoral processes'.

UNGA res. 50/185 (22 Dec. 1995), 'Strengthening the role of the United Nations in enhancing the effectiveness of the principle of periodic and genuine elections and the promotion of democratization'.

UNGA res. 50/178 (22 Dec. 1995), 'Situation of human rights in Cambodia'.

UNGA res. 50/86 (15 Dec. 1995), 'The situation of democracy and human rights in Haiti'.

United States of America: *Senate Election Law Guidebook 1996,* Senate, U.S. Government Printing Office, Washington, DC, 1996.

Valentino, Henry, 'Establishing and Maintaining Balanced Media Support for Free and Fair Elections', *Elections Today,* vol. 5, no. 1, Dec. 1994, 10.

Valentino, Henry, 'Guidelines for Media, Political Parties and Contesting Groups during Official Campaign Period for Municipal and Local Government Elections', drafted for use in Guyana, *Elections Today,* vol. 5, no. 1, Dec. 1994, 12-13.

von Meijenfeldt, Roel, 'Election Observation', Report of an ECDPM Workshop, Maastricht, The Netherlands, 14-16 June 1995, Arnold Bergstraesser Institut.

Weiser, Benjamin & McAllister, Bill, 'The Little Agency That Can't. Election-Law Enforcer is Weak by Design, Paralyzed by Division', *Washington Post,* 12 Feb. 1997.

Wiberg, Matti, *The Public Purse and Political Parties. Political Financing of Political Parties in Nordic Countries.* Finnish Political Science Association. 1991.